W9-BFL-591

THE BEST OF THE OLD
CHURCH
COOKBOOKS

by Florence Ekstrand

Welcome Press

Copyright © 1988
by Florence Ekstrand

ISBN 0-916871-10-X

Welcome Press
2701 Queen Anne Avenue North
Seattle, Washington 98109

Typesetting by Fjord Press
Manufactured in the United States of America

Cover stitchery by Corinne Otakie

Silhouette designs are from *1,001 Advertising Cuts from the Twenties and Thirties*,
Dover Publicatons, New York, used by permission.

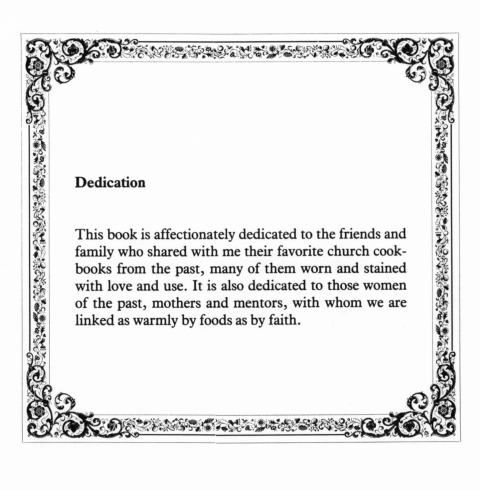

Dedication

This book is affectionately dedicated to the friends and family who shared with me their favorite church cookbooks from the past, many of them worn and stained with love and use. It is also dedicated to those women of the past, mothers and mentors, with whom we are linked as warmly by foods as by faith.

Contents

Introduction

The loaves and fishes were blessed and multiplied; the precise details were never recorded by the gospel writers.

But almost ever since, disciples—usually female—have been recording by measure, method and oven time things that have to do with food and faith. Who would venture to guess how many choir robes, altar cloths, pews, Sunday School rooms, youth camps and missionary enterprises have been financed by something called the church cookbook?

A few have been voluminous. *The Ann Arbor Cook Book*, put out in 1904 by the Ladies Aid Society of the Congregational Church of that Michigan city, has 606 pages and contains recipes for such things as Walnut Catsup and Cotton Batting Soup. It has a section on the handling of infectious diseases in the home and suggests that, besides washing the hands, "the hair, whiskers, face and clothes" of anyone leaving the sickroom should be brushed with a solution of bichloride of mercury and water. It also states that at that time "from 50 to 64 percent of the earnings of the laboring classes must be spent for food." And in writing about food values it endorses a saw of the time: " 'A well-fed horse can pull a heavy load,' and it is much the same with a man."

Some books have been pocket-sized, tiny collections thanks to the mimeograph machine and women who cut oilcloth covers with a pinking shears while someone else stapled the pages.

Most fall somewhere between. They are hardbound, softbound, printed, mimeographed, saddle-stitched, perfect-bound, comb-bound, spiral-bound, loose-leaf. Titles range from cutesy to direct (*Lutheran Favorites*). Many have Scripture verses referring to food, others carry household hints. Nearly every one has a recipe for Scripture Cake, and the pre–World War II books are almost sure to have a Recipe for Keeping a Husband Happy.

But one thing is certain: any woman who knew her recipe was going to be set down in black and white between book covers made sure she contributed her best. The best rye bread in the county, the best chocolate cake in the parish, these went into the church cookbook.

As women, we read our own history in the recipe books: the ordered days when the mother stayed home and made spiced peaches and long-simmering stews; the ingenious "make-do" of the Depression of the 1930s, when women drew on old skills to feed their families with bare-bones ingredients; the innovations of the World War II years, when women moved into men's jobs and discovered short-cut cooking; the expansive recipes of the 1950s as life started over with hats, gloves, dessert salads and triple-layer bars; the Sixties, when chickens were produced en masse and women, fearing change that came too fast, tried valiantly to recapture what had been.

With a few exceptions, recipes in this book are drawn from church cookbooks published before the 1970s. Like events, food needs time to be put into perspective.

We realized early on that we couldn't cover every kind of book. So for the most part we have drawn from books put out by women from backgrounds most familiar to us — those with northern European roots and traditions. Many are Scandinavian. Many of the books have a "Scandinavian Section." But for some of the older books, such a section would have been redundant, for the books themselves are peppered with foods straight out of a Norwegian past — or Swedish, or Finnish, or Danish.

We started out giving credit for each recipe that had a name after it. But it wasn't long before we discovered the same recipe turned up in dozens of books, some with small variations, others exactly alike. Some, like "Matrimonial Bars" and "Lazy Daisy Cake," were in almost every pre-1940 book. Even the ones with wildly imaginative names — Rickety Runkles, Jitters, Dandy Snaps, Dark Secrets, Ragged Robins, Golf Balls, Jim Jams, Maids of Honor, Yellow Jacket Frosting — even these might turn up in two and three books. We finally threw up our hands at matching all the names to recipes. I'd like to believe that most of them have already criss-crossed the country many times over on 3-by-5-inch cards tucked into letters to friends and relatives.

In almost every case we have printed the recipe exactly as it appeared in the original book. You'll find many directions to "put on fire" and "take off fire." The most frustrating direction will probably be "flour enough to roll." One page in a 1904 book has seven recipes for Ginger Cookies; only one specifies the amount of flour; five of them don't even mention flour! The cook was expected to *know* how the dough should feel. To a degree this is still true, for flour varies, type of shortening affects the amount of flour, temperature affects the feel of dough. Most recipes have room for a little variation.

And you'll want to adapt them to your own lifestyle. Salt can be cut or eliminated. Vegetable shortening and cholesterol-free oils instead of lard. Less butter (except in holiday cookies, where you will splurge!).

But even though broccoli and zucchini appeared in few books before the 1970s, there was a lot of good sense in their eating. Fish dishes abounded. Meat-stretching dishes, born of necessity and thrift, probably kept meat consumption at near the proper amount. Salads were a long time coming but all kinds of relishes brought extra vitamins to winter meals. If there weren't many vegetable recipes, it was likely because no one needed to be told how to boil carrots, peas, cabbage and all the rest.

There were no hors d'oeuvres in the early books. Eating was serious business. Lots of recipes for "Crazy Cake" and "Dump Cake," meaning you put all ingredients in a bowl and stirred. We've omitted the remarks at the end of recipes, like "Very tasty!" or "Guaranteed to please." Some recipes we debated about and left in, like Candlestick Salad. Others we debated about and left out, like "Chow Magne," which called for tomato soup.

The copyright on this book applies only to the book as a whole and the commentary. It's impossible to copyright recipes unless they are an absolutely unique creation using specific name-brand foods. So feel free to copy these and if you find one you especially like, include it in your own church cookbook. Who knows, it may have originated with one of your own long-forgotten relatives!

Compiling a book like this is more than a trip down Memory Lane. A lot more. I let the old names roll off my tongue — Jacobson, Johnson, Meckola, Kjelstrup, Miller, Schutz, Stenehjem, Lindbloom — and I almost feel their spirits clustered around my word processor, laughing, nudging each other, retying a loose apron string. I know it doesn't take a saint to write out a recipe for cream buns or apple fritters. But those same saints taught Sunday School, washed communion glasses, packed World Relief boxes, brought soup to shut-ins, led Bible studies, raised their substantial families — and more.

On the wall in front of me is a copy of an inscription on a memorial tablet: "Dietrich Bonhoeffer, a witness of Jesus Christ among his brethren. Born February 4, 1906, in Breslau. Died April 9, 1945, in Flossenburg."

In their own way, in their own time, these women were and are no less witnesses to Jesus Christ among those of their time and place. Belatedly, we send them our thanks and love.

Florence Ekstrand

Remembering the Early Years

Old Carrie Tack, wizened and sharp-eyed, ramrod-straight, wasn't much taller than the wheels of the buggy in which old Charley drove her to the country church long after other farmers had cars. Having deposited her he'd head the plodding horse home again. Someone else would give Carrie a ride home.

Carrie had to be at church early one Thursday afternoon a month, for she cooked the Ladies Aid coffee. The husband of one of the "serving ladies" would have hauled two or three large milk cans of scalding hot water from the creamery up the road, enough to cook the coffee and wash the dishes. But only Carrie mixed the coffee and raw egg and watched it as it foamed and rose in the granite-ware pots. Carrie knew just when to stir it down and when to draw it from the hottest surface of the big black range.

Our two-room school lay halfway between the church and the creamery, and some of my earliest school memories are of walking through the snow-encrusted cemetery to the basement door of the church, opening it and meeting a burst of warm, coffee-fragrant air, all mixed with the murmur of voices and laughter and clanking of cups on heavy china plates. We'd drop our tin lunch boxes in the entry and take off our overshoes. Then, like munchkins entering a turf that might or might not be friendly, we'd ease self-consciously into the Big Room. Ladies in black and navy blue felt hats sat in tight little rows with plates in their laps and seemed to be talking to no one in particular. (A friend tells of an aunt who excelled in this kind of talk: "She would carry on a non-stop conversation herself without missing a word of five separate conversations going on around her.")

There was an awful minute or two when the conversation stilled and the women turned to inspect this small invasion. Were my stockings sagging? Could they see how my long underwear was tucked inside my stockings? Was there ink on my lips? Dirt under my fingernails?

If we were lucky one of the hostesses would swoop down and lead us to the long table where a few plates remained, already made up with a sandwich (home-made white bread or maybe—oh, joy!—a bun) with chicken filling and a piece of yellow layer cake with chocolate frosting. If the hostesses were busy passing coffee ("Oh, just a few drops, a little påtår!") we'd go and stand in the kitchen doorway until someone noticed us and gave us plates. The nicety was understood: we had to be invited. We'd go through the Little Room, where the men who had come to pick up their wives (and give us children a ride home, too) were drinking coffee and talking corn prices and McCormick Deering tractors. We'd sit on the old daybed in the Baby Room. No one ever left their babies here; they would have smothered under the coats women piled here. We sat on top of the coats. Here we could giggle and slurp Watkins Orange Nectar and drop crumbs without anyone frowning at us.

We didn't know it then, of course, in those late 1920s, but we were at a turning point in history. My shoes were new and my lunch pail store-bought—no tin lard pail for me. My father looked trim and comfortable. My mother's new winter coat came below mid-calf but my older sisters were wearing skirts to their knees. That summer I would get a Boyish Bob—at the barber's, no less—and a couple years later we would wear Art Deco–print "beach pajamas" to Junior Missionary Society in the church basement. And when Sunday issues of the Chicago Herald and Examiner were dispatched to the seed-corn shed to start fires in the cast iron stove, I would sit by the hour devouring pictures of flappers in long roadsters, scarves flying, and stories of the curse of King Tut's tomb, and of Peter, the boy king of Rumania and of crown jewels and Rockefellers and Vanderbilts. And then—in 1929—of men jumping to their deaths from skyscraper windows.

And after that year, as my parents visited with other Swedish farm neighbors, I noticed more and more silences, followed by a sigh and then, "Well, things aren't like they used to be."

The Depression of the 1930s is one of those benchmarks in the lives of people my age and older. Few of us knew soup lines or any terrible privation; on the farms there were usually milk, eggs and a vegetable garden. But three straight years of drought, several years of rock-bottom farm prices, and the constant threat of foreclosure affected almost everyone. For some it meant merely belt-tightening, but for some it was heartbreaking.

Through a newspaper article, Rita Van Amber of Menominee, Wisconsin, asked for recipes and reminiscences of the Depression and these she incorporated into a poignant and moving book, *Recipes of the Great Depression of the 1930s.* Here is what some people remembered:

"Raisins were 5 cents a pound. But you seldom had the 5 cents. Double dip ice cream cones were 5 cents each but you didn't have the nickel. Butternuts were for the picking if you were smarter than the squirrel."

"Our cream check for two weeks was 50 cents."

"I remember my mother darning my father's and brother's socks with string from the grocery store."

"As if times weren't bad enough, all of our potatoes and canned goods were taken by the landlord for past-due rent. That winter we ate corn meal three times a day all winter long."

". . . garlic soup, which consisted of dry bread cubes, minced garlic, a dab of lard and boiling water poured over all."

"I took my baby along to work at the Lucas Cheese Factory . . . I was being paid $1.75 a week to work full days and I was fortunate to have a job."

But through all this the Church not only endured but continued to be the center of social as well as spiritual life. The pastor might be paid in eggs, potatoes, sides of pork and home-milled rye flour, but the old pipe organ was kept in tune, the women eked out egg money for mission projects, the men kept the coal furnace in repair, couples came to the parsonage to be married and brides received embroidered dish towels and ivory and green kitchenware at showers in the church basement.

"I always went to bridal showers," Helen (Munson) Hagen remembers, "whether I knew the bride or not, because there would be other kids there and there was always a big lunch." She also recalled Luther League, which was supposed to be a young people's organization but which practically everyone in the congregation attended.

"The program was a sort of amateur hour, I guess you'd say. We were all expected at some time to either sing, or recite a poem, or give a reading, or play an instrument. You didn't volunteer; you were asked, and you'd better do it. Again, lunch was a big event, especially when we got to be teenagers and would look over the boys at the end of the lunch line—and giggle."

There might even be time for some furtive exchanges. "Because if a farm boy wanted a date with a girl, he certainly wouldn't call her on the party line—the whole country would know about it. So it was to meet at church, or to casually stop in on the way to town to have some corn ground or something, and then to hope the girl would be around without her whole family to listen in."

Our mentors in those years—parents, pastors, teachers, Sunday School teachers—would probably not be what Martin Marty calls "summery" Christians. There wasn't a lot of "Praise the Lord!" or of holding hands aloft or of soul-searching to see if we truly "felt the joy."

Instead there was, I think, something deeper: a sense that in church or out, awake or asleep, at work or in play, one was in the presence of the Almighty God and it was a shelter, a rock, a foundation, a sure place. The Holy Spirit might be a nebulous and theological person of the Trinity to us, but Jesus Christ was one to be followed, one who made the impossible possible for us, one who was to be shared, one who empowered the "church of the practicers." We saw him in the lives of people who did what had to be done, who brought meals to the sick (whom they knew through listening in on the party line), who took the 50-cent cream check with a wry joke, who drew strength from the body of believers and, as much as possible, passed that strength on to the rest of us.

And a good thing they did. For barely had the rains come and the country begun to function again when the shadows of World War II lay across the land.

Remembering the War Years

You always remember where you were.

I remember a dimly lit house with Oriental rugs and an open stairway with a curved banister, a 1939 Bed and Breakfast without the breakfast. We were celebrating our first wedding anniversary and all the motels in Duluth were filled. We had seen the sign, had paid our money, moved in our bags and were returning from an exhilarating walk through a scarlet-leafed park; we had found a springer spaniel puppy and if we couldn't find the owner we were going to take him home. As we walked in the door, the woman nodded toward the living room where her husband sat close to the arch-shaped Philco. Her face looked older than it had an hour before.

"England has declared war on Germany," she whispered.

And then the late Sunday afternoon when I was trying to put one more round on the braided rug I was making. Cut, fold, braid and sew—surely I could make one round on this quiet afternoon. The radio had been blaring "The Yellow Rose of Texas" until in impatience I had snapped it off. I had just started the coffee when my husband, his father and brother walked in. They seemed strangely quiet.

"Have you had the radio on?" I shook my head. "Pearl Harbor has been bombed. We're at war with Japan."

In college we had written and talked a lot about cartels and international bankers, warlords and munition kings (the term "military-industrial complex" hadn't been invented yet), but war was something that happened somewhere else. We thought we could hold it at bay with words and prayers. Just before Memorial Day in 1938 I had written,

> Lord, we are young and life lies bright before us,
> Ours is the beauty of the field and tree;
> Ours is the service in Thy mighty kingdom,
> Bearing Thy peace past every furthest sea.
>
> Lord, wilt Thou spare us from a war-mad thinking,
> Take from our hand the dripping bayonet.
> Bury the cannon ere it reaps its harvest,
> Oh, may we know Thy peace is with us yet.
>
> Lord, we are young. We see fields green before us.
> Feel spring's bright promise on the fragrant breeze.
> Shape Thou our swords that we may plow these valleys,
> Bend Thou our spears that we may prune these trees.

Five years later, in 1943, I would write in memory of Harold Hagstrom, a confirmation classmate killed in action in North Africa:

We cannot go with flowers to a dear,
Familiar square of Minnesota sod
And say to friends, "A youth is sleeping here
Who pledged within this church his vows to God."
The sands of Africa are far, and seas
Deep-rent with death and danger bar the way,
But prayer transcends all distance, miles release
Their barriers and space is gone today.

Whether 'tis here or there he sleeps, God rest
A hero lying in a foreign land;
He who knew battle, let him now be blest
With peace that only comes within God's hand.
He who gave bravely, let him now be given
A thousand fold. And if he walked with fear,
Send joy instead; and may he know in heaven
His memory lives with those who knew him here.

And it would be 25 years later, in 1968, that I wrote for *Scope* magazine what it was like to have a son in Vietnam, that among the ragged edges of fear and loneliness God gives a state of mind that holds life together. And to a friend's question, "Does it last, this state of mind?" I wrote,

"I shook my head, for a slow painful change grows out of that peace. Week by week it grows, the agonizing feeling that every boy is your own. In this living room war where the dead lie stretched on a 21-inch television screen, I find myself weeping over the dead soldier, not because it might have been my son but simply because he was whoever he was. Each casualty headline jumps at me. Every parent's grief becomes my grief.

"Even prayer is difficult. Ask God to protect my son when the price might be another's life?

"And when the 14-year-old Viet Cong looks out at me from under his bandaged head I know he is my burden too.

"And then something else happens. Out of all this comes at last a conviction: however infinitesimal my part, I am compelled to add my effort to the struggle of peoples to understand each other and to find a way to work out differences short of war."

We had come into the Forties with hats and gloves that had to match our shoes, full of enthusiasm for self-improvement and the "fuller, more abundant life," much of which had to do with being asked to pour at the next coffee function. Girls wore bobby sox, young men wore zoot suits, "Mairzy Doats" came over the radio along with "I'd Like to Get You on a Slow Boat to China." Drive-in hamburger places with carhops sprang up all over.

Then came the war, draft boards, overseas mail, flags in windows with one, two, even three stars, often a gold star. New babies got war bonds and war stamps at showers. Volunteer air raid wardens planted Victory Gardens during the day. In 1943 home gardeners planted 20.5 million plots and produced a third of all the fresh vegetables in the nation. We recycled tin cans, silk and nylon stockings (provided we could get them in the first place), bacon grease, newspapers, tires, tinfoil, even empty toothpaste tubes.

And we prayed.

Recipe books were published by churches during World War II years, but there were only fleeting references to the war. But Jane Quanbeck has her Grandmother Anderson's little book issued by the Watkins Company to help cooks cope with rationing of meat, butter, sugar, and the absence of many products containing these. (Coffee was also rationed.)

"At two red points a pound, fortified vegetable margarine is an excellent butter substitute," begins a section on extending butter. There is a recipe for whipping butter with a gelatine and condensed milk mix. There is emphasis on using corn syrup instead of sugar, baking sugarless cakes, saving sugar in "putting up" fruit. There are several pages of hints and recipes for stretching meat, many of which we use today as a matter of course—stews, soups, baked stuffed vegetables, meat loaves, economy cuts. It urges the use of fish, chicken, eggs, cheese and dried peas and beans instead of meats on the ration list. Liver, heart, kidneys, sweetbreads were not rationed. (Our first experiences with variety meats like kidneys and sweetbreads were not always happy ones!)

Homemakers were also urged to save paper. "Waste paper is used to make more than 100,000 items for the Armed Forces, including shell containers, blood plasma containers and K-ration cartons."

Reclaimed tin was urgently needed for "making tin plate for more cans, for solder, and many military uses such as tanks and airplanes." We were urged to save kitchen fats for making gunpowder and sulfa drugs.

Today, as garbage landfills eat up precious land and cities and communities find themselves in horrendous crises, we can act as responsibly as we did in the war years: recycle paper, cans and glass and work to have plastic containers banned. As for kitchen fats, women in many churches are reviving their grandmothers' art and making fine soap for relief shipments overseas.

Remembering the Fifties

Women of the Eighties find it hard to understand why the women's movement, which made such gains in the first 30 years of this century, accomplished so little in the next 30 years. With such victories as women's suffrage and the end to child labor and women's sweatshop employment, why didn't property rights and equal pay for equal worth come next? What happened to the momentum?

Certainly the Depression of the Thirties was a factor. Women worked at trying to hang on to their jobs, at saving their husband's business, keeping the farm, putting food on the table, making over hand-me-downs, holding on to some semblance of the good life. There was little of time or energy to fight for anything else.

World War II occupied most of the 1940s. Women worked alongside men in defense plants and industry. It wasn't a matter of rights, it was manpower — workerpower. Women learned to weld, to drive trucks, to cut meat in butcher shops. They ferried planes and served as officers in branches that did the same work men would have done. And those of us who stayed home raising children and gardens tied our hair up in white dish towels, bandana style, like Rosie the Riveter. Slacks became accepted dress outside of church and formal occasions. Women who had never worked outside the home a day in their lives brought home paychecks and bought War Bonds and balanced their own checkbooks for the first time. Farm help, even farm sons were drafted; women drove tractors and delivered calves and lambs.

And then the war ended. By the time the dust had settled and the lucky ones had begun to pick up the pieces, we were almost into the 1950s.

On the very eve of the Fifties, Russia exploded her first atomic bomb. Later, Nikita Krushchev said, "We will bury you." Halfway through the decade a Montgomery, Alabama, seamstress would refuse to give up her seat on the bus. By the end of the decade Joseph McCarthy would have risen and fallen, and a hip-swinging, guitar-playing singer on the Ed Sullivan Show would have changed the face of the world's music.

But there are some who say that it was the French fashion designers who, in a classic example of the tail wagging the dog, did more than anyone else to make the Fifties what they were.

German occupation had of course suspended the influence of French couturiers for the duration. And American designers had been forced to work within the confines of wartime restrictions on material: no skirts wider at the bottom than 72 inches, no hem deeper than two inches, one pocket only, no wide belts, no cuffs on coats.

But no sooner had the war ended than Paris burst on the fashion scene with clothes absolutely feminine — full, flowing silhouettes, longer, swirling skirts, frilly touches, feminine accessories. Mills turned to luxuriant fabrics again. And the time was right. The men were home and the women wanted to look like women again, to be women, to be what they had dreamed of being through the Forties — someone with a husband, children and a split-level house.

And so they were. All over the land housing developments sprang up. Men who had learned to build in the Seabees built their own three-bedroom, two-bath homes on acre plots at the edge of town. We looked down our noses at houses that looked like "little boxes, little boxes," but we were happy enough to move into them. Sandlot games gave way to organized Little Leagues. We got automatic washers, brush rollers, poodle cuts, drive-in movies, hula hoops, crinoline petticoats that had to be starched and dried in great circles on the lawn. (Some high schools outlawed them: they created such gridlock in the halls it slowed down the passing of classes.) Television was no longer a novelty. In 1950 there were TV sets in 3.1 million homes; five years later there were 32 million sets out there. In 1956 we spent $15.6 million buying and repairing TV sets. All things grew — and grew, and grew.

No less the churches. We built education wings and sponsored home mission congregations. Women who had helped build their own houses now taped and sanded and spackled and painted Sunday School rooms and tried to connect theology to carpeting. Having sold enough cookbooks to buy chairs for the rooms, we worked just as hard to fill the rooms with children.

But it wasn't surface growth only. Church life fostered personal spiritual growth and out-reaching evangelism. Community Bible studies and neighborhood Bible Clubs for children sprang up. We talked a lot about consecration, dedication; maybe not as much about application. And as this comfortable decade progressed, there was sometimes heard a sort of "success theology"—give your life to Christ and prepare to prosper financially and live successfully.

It is said that periods of spiritual renewal are usually followed by periods of social reforms, but the reforms may not always be what the spiritual renewers had in mind.

Maybe that's the way it was with the Fifties. I have in my collection a cookbook put out in the Fifties, at about the time that the Chiffon Cake burst on our horizon and the Los Angeles housewife built the first backyard bomb shelter. The book is filled with things like Double-Decker Pork Chops, Peach Party Loaf, Marshmallow Delight.

Little could we know then that a decade later we would be thanking God for books like *Diet for a Small Planet*, or that considerations like the politics of hunger would, for the rest of our lives, affect the way we looked at food.

Remembering the Sixties

Even for those who weren't yet born in the Sixties, one word comes to mind: protest.

Not that there weren't great strides made in this country—the first American in Space at the beginning of the decade and the first man to set foot on the moon at the end of the decade. There was President Kennedy's New Frontier, and the Peace Corps with 18,000 enlisting in the first year. There was an awakening awareness of health and fitness; jogging was called "a craze." Retirement villages sprang up, but so did miniskirts, singles clubs and computerized dating.

But on November 22, 1963, church bells tolled and the nation mourned a slain president. The Vietnam involvement grew into a brutal war. Protest against the war escalated on a simultaneous path with civil rights marches. There were sit-ins and counter protests. Doves, hawks, flower children, hippies, dropouts, communes, pot came into the language. Students protested the war, dropouts protested control, children protested discipline.

But middle-aged housewives protested, too. Women who had worn the hats and white gloves, fashioned the jelled salads, organized clubs and run the PTA, mimeographed cookbooks, taught Sunday School and marched their starched and polished children into the pew each Sunday morning—we protested, too.

Mostly it was a silent, inward-turning protest. First it may have been a protest against a mindless, undeclared war that took our sons. It was a protest against all that had turned our ordered, settled world of the Fifties upside down. Like Scarlett, we craved the unchanging soil of a spiritual Tara. And because in our need God, in the power of the Trinity, revealed Himself as a force beyond even the bomb, and because we found Him in the midst of pain and in sharing the pain of others, we protested the form, order, organization and other niceties that had kept us so comfortable in the Fifties and that seemed so hollow in the Sixties.

In Spokane Helen Landsverk sang gentle, funny songs with a bite:

Find me a church with a good cup of coffee,
Find me a church where the In crowd goes,
Find me a church where the women aren't bossy,
One where the members all wear the right clothes.

Find me a church with the right kind of pastor,
Find me one with a quiet wife.
Find me a pastor who preaches must faster,
Find me one who will stay here for life.

Find me a church with the right kind of neighbors,
Find me a church in the right part of town,
Find me a church where we rest from our labors,
Where we can wear all the stars in our crown.

Find me a church with the right kind of preaching,
Sprinkled with stories and beautiful prose.
Find me a church with some comfortable teaching,
Not too far out and that everyone knows.

Find me a church with the right kind of singing,
One with an organ with carillon chimes.
Find me a church where the choir is clinging
To dignified songs with solid old rhymes.

Find me a church where there's plenty of money,
Without any mortgage or pledges to sign,
One that is flowing with just milk and honey —
When you find it I'll join, it'll suit me just fine!

Sometimes I wrote lyrics for her melodies:

Dear Mr. Ashton, figures make it clear
You have not worshipped with us for almost half a year.
I'm sure you will agree this does not please the Lord.
Yours very truly, Chairman of the Board.

Dear Mr. Chairman, I was pleased to learn
Of your very neatly mimeographed concern.
The i's were sharply dotted, the print was very bright
And you hand-wrote my number in the upper right.

But were you there when I touched the shroud,
And did you hear when I cried aloud?
And when I bled and nearly died,
Was it you who passed on the other side?
Where are you when the cities burn?
Who am I, and where shall I turn?

But thank you, Mr. Chairman, for your mimeographed concern,
Thank you for your mimeographed concern,

But for all the pain of the Sixties, there was a catharsis about those years. There was a jolting, unnerving awareness that we had paid lip — yes, and heart — service to the risen Christ but had not seen Him in our brothers or sisters, whether it was the blacks of Selma, our own native American neighbors, the homosexuals among us, the growing number of homeless, the dropouts, the rebellious, the disenfranchised, the hurting. We woke to something dark inside ourselves that we had never put a name to; it was not so much prejudice as indifference to prejudice. Facing it brought a measure of healing and, prudently, we thought, we went about making amends. Sometimes we fell on our faces.

The first black children, Pansy and Edna, came by voluntary busing to my daughter's fourth grade classroom. We invited them for a birthday party and they came. Elated, we drove them home and asked Pansy's mother if the girls could go with us on an all-Sunday outing to Whidbey Island.

"Thank you," said Pansy's mother in a no-nonsense tone, "but the girls both attend Sunday school at our church and I really wouldn't like them to miss a Sunday."

A BOOK
of TRIED RECIPES
and how to use Them

Breads

*In the 1904 "Ann Arbor Cook Book"
prepared by the Ladies Aid Society of the
Congregational Church in Ann Arbor,
Michigan, Mrs. J. B. Wheeler of Peoria,
Illinois, contributed this "Prison Mission
Brown Bread." She wrote, "This recipe was
given me by the wife of our United States
Prison Missionary, Rev. W. D. A.
Matthews, Onarga, Illinois, who is doing so
much for the welfare of prisoners."*

Prison Mission Brown Bread

1 pt sour milk
1 cup corn meal
1 cup graham flour
1 cup white flour
1 tsp salt
1 tsp soda
½ cup molasses

Steam two hours and bake one hour in a
2-quart basin. (Use a well-oiled 2-quart
casserole set in a pan of hot water. After
the first two hours remove the water and
bake about 45 minutes, all at 325 degrees.)

White Bread

1 pkg fast rising yeast
½ cup warm water
½ cup sugar
2 cups milk
5 T shortening
4 tsp salt
3 cups water
16 cups flour

Soak the yeast in the lukewarm water, add
one teaspoon sugar. Let stand about 15
minutes or until yeast is light and foamy.
Scald the milk. Put into large crock, sugar,
salt and shortening. Pour hot milk over
this mixture and stir until shortening is
melted and sugar and salt dissolved. Add 3
cups water and 6 cups flour. Beat until
smooth. Add the yeast and beat well. Then
add about 10 cups of flour. Stir in the first
few cups but as mixture becomes stiff
knead in the remaining flour. Knead until
dough is soft and smooth and does not
stick to the hands. This takes several
minutes. Grease the dough. Cover with a
tight lid and set it in a warm place. Let rise
until light. Knead the dough in the crock.
Let rise a second time. This time put the
dough on the bread board and knead
lightly and shape into loaves. Grease the
loaves and let rise in a warm place until
light. Bake in a moderate oven about 1
hour. This amount makes six large loaves.

*About yeast: Pre-1960 recipes called for either
dry yeast or compressed yeast. Today's
envelopes of granulated yeast are equal to
about half a cake of compressed yeast. Use
two envelopes of yeast where one cake is called
for, three envelopes where two cakes are called
for. Dry yeast needs a mix of warm water,
sugar and flour to begin acting.*

Never Fail White Bread

1 qt water (lukewarm)
2 cakes Fleishman's yeast
4 lbs flour
4 oz sugar
4 oz lard, melted
1 oz salt

Dissolve yeast in the water. Add sugar,
salt, melted shortening to 4 lbs of flour,
then water. Mix and knead thoroughly.
Let it rise 45 minutes. Punch down, let rise
1 hour and 15 minutes. Punch down until
all air is worked out of the dough. Make
into loaves, let rise about 30 minutes and
bake. Do not keep dough too warm, just
room temperature, during the rising
period. You will have delicious homemade
bread.

22

Crusty French Bread

1 T shortening
1 T salt
2 tsp sugar
1 cup boiling water
1 cup cold water
1 cake compressed yeast

Mix salt, sugar and shortening — pour over the boiling water and then the cold water. Blend in the yeast. Add 5½ cups of flour gradually. Mix well. Knead for 5 minutes. Place in a greased bowl and let rise 1½ hours. Place on flour board and form into 2 long thin loaves. Place on a cookie sheet making 3 diagonal slashes with a knife in each loaf. Let rise 1 hour. Then brush with unbeaten egg white. Bake at 400° for 15 minutes, then at 350° for 45 minutes. Cool uncovered for a hard crust.

Whole Wheat Bread

2 cups milk, scalded
5 tsp salt
⅓ cup honey or sorghum
2 cups lukewarm water
3 yeast cakes
10 cups whole wheat flour

Scald the milk and add 5 tsp salt and the honey or sorghum. Dissolve yeast cakes in water. Combine milk and water, and add 5 cups of whole wheat flour. Then add ⅓ cup melted shortening. Then add remaining flour.

Mother's Rye Bread

In evening: Heat 3 cups of potato water. Add 2 mashed potatoes, 2T sugar. Dissolve 1 cake yeast foam in a half cup of lukewarm water. Add to the first ingredients. Cover well and leave till morning.

In morning: Add flour to make sponge. Put aside to raise. When double in bulk add ½ cup molasses, 2 T lard, a handful of brown sugar, and some salt. Then add rye flour to make a stiff dough. Knead or handle with white flour. Let raise till double in bulk. Form into loaves, put in pans, and raise till double in bulk. Bake in moderate oven.

Root Bear Rye Bread

1 qt Root Beer
½ cup lard
2 T salt
⅔ cup dark molasses
2 pkg yeast
½ cup warm water
3 cups rye flour (unsifted)
7 cups white flour (presifted)

Heat root beer and lard until lard is melted. Add salt and molasses. Add yeast dissolved in warm water. Add 3 cups rye flour and 3 cups white flour. Beat until smooth; keep on adding more white flour and beating and mixing until you have added about 7 cups of white flour in all. Place on a mixing board and knead until smooth and can be handled easily. Place in a greased bowl. Set in a warm place covered. Let rise until doubled. Knead down; let rise again. Divide into 4 portions; make into loaves. Let rise slightly over top of pan. Bake in moderate oven 325° for 40 minutes. Remove from pans and cool on rack. When cool, may put in plastic bags and freeze.

Sweet Dough Buns

2 pkg dry yeast
1 T sugar
1 cup lukewarm water
1 cup milk
3 eggs, beaten
½ cup sugar
6 T shortening
1 tsp salt
7 cups sifted flour

Dissolve yeast and 1 T sugar in lukewarm water. Scald milk. Add shortening, sugar and salt. Cool to lukewarm. Add 2 cups flour to make a batter. Add yeast and beaten eggs. Beat wll. Add remaining flour or enough to make a soft dough. Knead lightly and place in greased bowl. Cover and set in warm place, free from draft. Let rise until doubled in bulk, about 2 hours. When light, punch dough down and shape according to directions for Swedish Tea Ring, Filled Coffee Ring, or Cinnamon Buns.

REMEDY FOR COLD FEET.

Every night on going to bed, dip the feet in shallow, cold water, two or three times, quickly, then rub briskly with a coarse towel till dry; then take hold of each end of the towel and draw it back and forth through the hollow of the foot until a glow is excited.

FOR BILIOUS HEADACHE.

Dissolve and drink two teaspoonfuls of finely-powdered charcoal in one-half a tumbler of water. It will relieve in a few moments; take a Seidlitz powder one hour afterwards.

CURE FOR TOOTHACHE (SURE).

Powdered alum and fine salt, equal quantities, apply to the tooth. A better cure is to hold a root in your hand about one foot above your head; the root of the tooth is best for the purpose.

HOW SHE MAKES BREAD.

"Bread!" exclaimed a Vassar College girl. "Bread! Well, I should say I can make bread. We studied that in our first year. You see, the yeast ferments, and the gas thus formed permeates everywhere and transforms the plastic material a clearly obvious atomic structure, and then—" "But is the plastic material you speak of?" "Oh! that is only called the sponge." "But how do you make the ge?" Why, you don't make it; the cook always at-ls to that. Then we test the sponge with the thermome-nd hydrometer and a lot of other instruments, the names of which I don't remember, and then hand it back to the ok, and I don't know what she does with it then, but she National yeast and when it comes on the table it is just d."

How She Makes Bread

"Bread!" exclaimed a Vassar College girl. "Bread! Well, I should say I can make bread. We studied that in our first year. You see, the yeast ferments, and the gas thus formed permeates everywhere and transforms the plastic material into a clearly obvious atomic structure and then — "

"But what is the plastic material you speak of?"

"Oh, that is commonly called the sponge."

"But how do you make the sponge?"

"Why, you don't make it, the cook always sees to that. Then we test the sponge with the thermometer and the hydrometer and a lot of other instruments, the names of which I can't remember, and then we hand it back to the cook and I don't know what she does with it then, but she uses National yeast and when it comes on the table it is just splendid!"

–1886 cookbook
(Excerpt on opposite page)

Russian Raisin Bread

1 pkg yeast, compressed or dry
¼ cup lukewarm water
1¼ cups scalded milk
2 eggs, beaten
4 T sugar
4 T melted shortening
2 tsp salt
½ lemon juice and rind
⅛ tsp nutmeg
1½ cups seeded raisins
6 cups flour

Soften yeast in the lukewarm water. Scald milk and cool to lukewarm. Add 1½ cups of flour and beat until smooth. Add the softened yeast. Beat until well mixed. Cover and let stand until sponge is light and bubbly. Stir down and beat in the eggs, one at a time, beating well after each addition. Add rest of ingredients as listed down to the flour. Add enough flour to make a nice dough. Let rise until double in size. Then knead it down again. Let rise again after which mold into loaves and let rise until double in size. Bake at 350° about 50 minutes according to size of loaves.

4 Hour Parker House Rolls

1 cake yeast
½ cup lukewarm water or milk
⅓ cup lard
⅓ cup sugar
1½ tsp salt
1½ cups scalded milk
4 cups flour
1 beaten egg

Dissolve yeast in lukewarm water or milk. Pour the scalded milk over the lard, sugar and salt. Add 2 cups of flour and stir well. Add egg and yeast. Then add remaining flour and stir well. Let rise, punch down and let rise again. Roll out, cut with cutter. Brush butter on ½ and fold over. Let rise. Bake 25 minutes in 350° oven.

Cold Water Buns

In the morning make a sponge of 2 cups flour, 2 cups cold water, 1 cup sugar, ½ cup lard and a tsp salt, 1 cake yeast. Let stand all day in not too warm place. Make the buns in the evening and let them rise over night. Don't make them very large. Put them quite a space apart. Bake in a hot oven in the morning.

Butter Horns

4 cups flour
1 cake yeast
¾ cups butter or lard
1 cup warm milk
2 eggs
½ cup sugar
½ tsp salt

Blend butter into flour. Add beaten eggs. Dissolve yeast in warm milk and add to first mixture. Add sugar and salt and let stand over night. In the morning, divide dough into 4 parts. Roll out as for pie crust and cut in eight wedge shaped pieces. Spread with butter and roll up toward the corner. Bake at 300°.

Clover Leaf Rolls

1 cup milk
2 T sugar
2 T Spry (shortening)
1 tsp salt
½ cake compressed yeast
¼ cup lukewarm water
1 beaten egg
3½ cups flour (or more)

Heat milk. Add sugar, salt and Spry. Let cool to luke warm. Then add yeast dissolved in water. Add egg and flour. Beat hard with a spoon. Let rise to double in size. Shape into clover leaf rolls. (Lay 3 balls of dough size of small walnuts in greased muffin tins.) Let rise to double in size and bake in oven 350° 25 to 40 minutes.

Refrigerator Rolls

1 cup milk
¼ cup sugar
¼ cup fat
1 tsp salt
3 cups flour
1 egg
1 cake compressed yeast

Melt fat in ½ of milk. Add sugar and salt. Add remaining milk and cool until luke warm. Add yeast and beaten egg. Stir well. Work in flour and let rise to double bulk. Knead lightly. Place in bowl and store in refrigerator. When ready for use, knead lightly, shape, and allow to double in bulk before baking. Bake in hot oven about 15 minutes.

Three Day Buns

1 yeast cake
1½ cups lukewarm water
1 cup sugar
½ cup lard
2 cups cold water
1 tsp salt
Flour

At noon soak a yeast cake in lukewarm water. In the evening stir in flour, cover and leave till morning. In the morning add sugar, lard, and cold water. Add salt, knead until it does not stick to fingers. Let rise and work down at noon. Let rise again. In the evening make into balls about 1½ inches in diameter, put in pans, leaving plenty of space. Bake in a hot oven. This recipe makes about 60 buns.

Hot Cross Buns

1 cake yeast
2 T sugar
2 cups milk
7½ cups flour
½ cup butter
⅔ cups sugar
2 eggs
½ cup currants
½ tsp salt
2 tsp cinnamon

Dissolve yeast and sugar in lukewarm milk. Add 3¼ cups flour to make sponge. Beat until smooth. Let rise until light, add butter and sugar creamed, eggs well beaten, currants, and balance of flour or enough to make soft dough. Knead and let rise until light, or about 2 hours. Shape with hands into small flat buns, grease tops, place about 2 inches apart in pans. Let rise till very light. Bake about 20 minutes. These buns can be made into hot cross buns by cutting a cross in tops & frosting lightly with powdered sugar icing.

Ice Box Rolls

1 qt scalded milk
1 cup lard
1 cup mashed potatoes
¾ cups sugar
1 cake compressed yeast
½ cup warm water
1 qt flour
2 tsp baking powder
1 tsp soda
1 tsp salt

Scald milk, add lard, when luke warm add mashed potatoes, sugar, cake of compressed yeast dissolved in ½ cup warm water, 1 qt flour, 2 tsp baking powder and soda. Let stand 3 hours. Add salt and flour enough to roll out very thin. This dough can be kept in ice box and used as needed.

Butterscotch Bites

½ cup warm water
2 pkg dry yeast
¾ cup lukewarm water
¼ cup sugar
1 tsp salt
2 eggs
½ cup shortening
3¼ cups all-purpose flour

Prepare 24 muffin cups by mixing 1 tsp butter & 2 tsp brown sugar & ¼ water in each. Arrange walnut halves on top of mixture. Soak yeast in ½ cup warm water for 5 minutes. Combine milk, sugar, salt, shortening, egg, 2 cups of sifted flour, & softened yeast mixture in mixing bowl. Beat 2 minutes with electric mixer or by hand until smooth. Add remaining sifted flour. Beat 2 more minutes (low speed) until thick & smooth. Drop 1 T batter in each prepared muffin cup. Let rise in warm place (80°–85°) until doubled in bulk (30–40 minutes). Bake at 375° F. for 18–20 minutes. Invert on baking sheet and let stand a few minutes before removing. Serve warm.

Some of the best recipes are hand-written in the back of books or on blank pages here and there. This one is from a book used many years ago by Aunt Josie Johnson (Mrs. August Johnson)

Irene's Shortcake

2 cups flour
½ tsp salt
4 tsp baking powder
1 T sugar
⅓ cup shortening
½ cup rich milk
1 well-beaten egg

Sift dry ingredients together. Beat egg, add to milk. Mix shortening in flour as for piecrust. Add and mix in liquid. Pat down in greased cake pan. Bake at 400° 10 to 20 minutes.

Plain Johnny Cake

1 T sugar
1 T butter or lard
1 egg
1 tsp soda
2 cups sour milk or buttermilk
1 tsp salt
1 cup cornmeal
1 cup white flour

Mix all dry ingredients, add melted butter, beaten egg and sour milk. Bake in dripping pan in moderate oven.

Corn Bread Sticks

1½ cups corn meal
¾ cup boiling water
½ tsp soda
1 cup butter milk
1 egg
1 tsp salt
1 T melted butter

Scald meal in hot water, add soda to buttermilk and pour half of this into scalded meal and stir well. Add egg, beat well, and add remainder of milk, salt and melted butter. Cook in well greased bread-stick pans.

Quaker Muffins

1 cup rolled oats
1 cup flour
3 T sugar
4 tsp baking powder
½ tsp salt
1 cup milk
1 egg
1 T butter

Scald milk, pour on rolled oats and let stand before mixing. Mix and sift dry ingredients to the rolled oats and milk mixture. Add beaten egg and melted butter. Beat well and bake in muffin pans half hour in a moderately hot oven.

Yield: 12 muffins.

Twin Mountain Muffins

¼ cup shortening
¼ cup sugar
1 egg
2 cups flour
3 tsp baking powder
½ tsp salt
¾ cup milk

Cream sugar & shortening together. Add beaten egg, sift flour, B.P. and salt together and add alternately with the milk. Bake in greased muffin tins in a hot oven.

7 Week Refrigerator Bran Muffins

2 cups boiling water
2 cups bran flakes
    Soak and cool.
1 cup shortening
3 cups white sugar
4 beaten eggs
1 qt buttermilk
5 cups white flour
5 tsp soda
1 tsp salt
4 cups Kellogg's All Bran

Cream fat & sugar. Add eggs. Add buttermilk & soaked 100% bran flakes. Sift dry ingredients & add with All Bran. Mix until moist. Keeps 6 to 7 weeks in refrigerator. Real tasty. Bake at 400° F.

Muffins for Two

1 T butter melted
1 T sugar
1 cup flour
1 tsp baking powder
1 egg
½ cup sweet milk
1 pinch salt
Any chopped fruit

Mix well and bake in hot oven for 15 minutes.

Cocoa Ginger Bread

Mix together 2 rounded T cocoa, ¾ cup sugar, 1 tsp ginger, ½ tsp cloves, ½ tsp nutmeg, ½ tsp cinnamon. Add 1 tsp soda to 1 cup sour milk. Sift three times 1½ cup bread flour, ½ tsp salt. Add milk and flour alternately to other ingredients. Then add 4 T melted shortening & last 1 unbeaten egg. Bake in moderate oven about 35 minutes. Serve with whipped cream.

Dutch Bread

1 cup sugar
1 egg
2 T butter
1½ cup sour milk
⅓ lb raisins
¼ tsp baking powder
1 tsp soda
1½ cups graham flour
1½ cups white flour
½ cup nuts

Mix in order given and bake in loaf pan in moderate oven for 1 hour.

My Favorite Cream Biscuits

2 cups flour
2 tsp baking powder
1 tsp salt
Sift all together

Make a hole in center and pour in ½ cup sweet cream and enough sweet milk to make a soft dough. Put enough flour on board to handle and knead lightly. Cut and Bake at about 400° F. for 15 minutes in quick oven.

ENDORSED
BY
PURE
FOOD
EXPERTS

For best results in baking from the recipes in this book you should use flour made by Clinard Milling Company.

MOTHER'S CHOICE
A High-Grade Plain Flour, or
MORNING GLORY
A Superior Self-Rising

Order From Your Grocer

CLINARD

MILLING

COMPANY

HIGH POINT, N. C.

"Soliciting Your Patronage"

The "angels" of the early church cookbooks were the advertisers, who helped pay the printing bill in the hope their message would be read each time the book was laid open on the kitchen table.

In 1901, when steamboats carried freight and farm goods up and down Puget Sound, La Conner, Washington, was a thriving trade center. That year the Ladies of the Catholic Mite Society brought out a cookbook which has recently been reissued (from the original plates) by Dick Fallis of nearby Mount Vernon.

The advertisements are a picture of the times and of village life. Parsons and Gilbert Millinery reminded readers that they carried "hats, flowers, ribbons, laces, feathers, satins, chiffons, stamped linens, sofa cushions, Battenberg patterns and braids, embroidery and rope silks." Nelson and Pearson carried "Smoked Salmon and Herring, Salt Salmon and Salmon Bellies, French, Norwegian and American Sardines, Kelsno and Norway Herring, Norway Anchovies and Fish Balls, Norway Macadammu Cheese, Swedish Summerset, Heinz's Pickles, Chow Chow and Mustard in Bottles and Bulk." We should find such a shop today!

Others advertised wagons, buggies, carriages, farming tools, cook stoves, harness, saddles, bridles, robes and whips as well as harness repair.

And James Gaches, whose Victorian mansion still crowns the hill above the village, concluded his general store's full-page ad somewhat testily: "If others can sell goods at cost, I certainly can and will appreciate your patronage."

Orange Bread

Rind 2 oranges
½ cup sugar
3 cups flour
2 T orange juice
2 T melted shortening
¼ cup sugar
1 cup water
1 cup milk
1 egg
4 tsp B.P.
1 tsp salt
1 cup nuts

Cut rind fine and add 1 cup water. Bring to a boil. Drain. Repeat. Drain again. Add ½ cup water and ½ cup sugar to rind and let simmer till rind is tender. Cool slightly and add milk. Add the flour, B.P., salt and ¼ cup sugar sifted together while rind mixture is still warm. Add beaten egg, juice, shortening and nuts. Beat till smooth. Let stand a few minutes. Bake 1 hour at 350.

Orange Peel Loaf

1 cup sugar
1 cup water
Ground peel of 2 oranges
1 egg
½ tsp salt
⅓ cup sugar
1 cup milk
3 cups flour
3 tsp baking powder

Boil sugar, water and orange peel till it hairs or is nearly dry. Remove from fire. Have egg beaten with sugar and salt and add to above mixture while hot. Add milk, flour, and baking powder. Chopped nuts may be added. Bake in slow oven.

Cranberry-Orange Bread

Sift together:
    2 cups flour
    1 cup sugar
    1½ tsp baking powder
    1 tsp soda
    1 tsp salt

Stir into dry ingredients:
    1 cup raw cranberries (halved)
    1 cup chopped walnuts
    1 tsp grated orange rind

Combine juice of one orange, 2 T butter plus enough hot water to make ¾ cup. Cool and add 1 beaten egg. Add to dry ingredients, stirring just until moistened. Let stand in pan 20 minutes before baking. Bake in well greased 9×5×3 inch pan at 350° for 50-60 minutes.

Prune Bread

1 lb prunes
2 cups sugar
½ cup butter
1 tsp cinnamon
½ tsp nutmeg
¼ tsp cloves
1 tsp salt
4 cups flour
2 T cocoa
2 tsp soda
2 eggs

Soak prunes over night in water to cover; drain, retaining 2 cups of liquid. Pit and chop prunes. Put in sauce pan with 2 cups water, sugar, butter, cinnamon, nutmeg, cloves and salt. Cook 5 minutes. Cool. Sift flour and cocoa and soda. Beat eggs and stir liquid into dry ingredients. Bake in two 5×9 loaf pans at 350 for 1 hour. Better if allowed to mellow.

Bran Loaf

1 cup brown sugar
1 T butter
2 cups sour milk
2 cups white flour
1 tsp baking powder
1 tsp soda
1 pinch salt
2 cups bran
1 cup raisins or dates

Cream butter and sugar, add milk. Add flour which has been mixed and sifted with baking powder, salt, and soda. Then add bran and fruit cut fine. Bake in a moderate oven for about 1 hour. This makes 2 small or 1 large loaf.

Blueberry Bread

1 cup sugar
2 eggs
3 T Mazola oil
    Beat together.
1 cup milk
3 cups flour
4 tsp baking powder
½ cup nuts
1 tsp salt
1 cup blueberries drained (fresh or frozen)

Fold in berries after beating is done. Bake at 350° F. for 50-60 minutes or longer.

Carrot Nut Bread

1 cup sugar
¾ cup salad oil
1½ cup flour
1 tsp baking powder
1 tsp soda
¼ tsp salt
1 tsp cinnamon
1 cup grated raw carrots
½ cup nuts
2 eggs

Mix sugar & oil. Add sifted dry ingredients. Then add carrots. Add eggs one at a time. Mix well. Bake in a loaf pan 55 minutes at 375° F.

Banana All-Bran Nut Bread

½ cup sugar
¼ cup shortening
1 egg well beaten
1 cup Kellogg's All-Bran
1½ cup flour
½ tsp soda
2 T water
½ cup chopped nuts
1½ cups mashed bananas
1 tsp vanilla
2 tsp baking powder
1 tsp salt

Cream shortening and sugar well. Add egg and All-Bran. Sift flour, B.P., soda and salt together. Mix nuts with flour mixture and add alternately with mashed bananas, to which the water has been added. Stir in the vanilla. Pour into greased loaf pan. Let stand 30 minutes. Bake at 375 for one hour. Let cool before it is cut.

Date and Nut Bread

1 cup dates
2 cups boiling water
2 tsp soda
1½ cups sugar
2 T butter or crisco
2 eggs
4 cups flour
1 tsp salt
2 tsp vanilla
1 cup nut meats

Pour boiling water over dates and soda and let cool. Cream sugar and butter and add to date mixture. Add eggs, flour, salt, vanilla and nut meats. Put in well greased tin cans (size 2½) filling them ⅔ full. Bake in moderate oven about 1 hour. This makes 4 cans.

Gum Drop Bread

Rinds of 2 oranges
2 cups sugar
2 cups milk
2 eggs
¼ tsp salt
½ cup chopped walnuts or pecans if desired
2 T butter
2 cups flour
2 cups graham flour
4 tsp baking powder
1 cup chopped gum drops (various bright colors preferred)
1 cup chopped dates (optional)

Boil orange rinds in plenty of water till tender; drain, rinse well, add a little water to these, and when boiling again add half the sugar. Continue to simmer until thick, then cool and put through food chopper. Mix with other ingredients as you would a cake, and pour into greased loaf pans. Let stand 20 minutes before baking in a slow oven for 1 hour. (Note: 2 cups of sugar are used — 1 in the orange rind and 1 in the batter. If prepared candied peel is used, only 1 cup of sugar is used in this recipe.) Makes 2 large loaves.

Yeast Cakes

1 qt fresh buttermilk
Yellow corn meal
3 yeast cakes
½ tsp ginger

Let buttermilk come to a boil, stir in all the corn meal possible and let cool. Add yeast cakes that have been soaked in a little lukewarm water and then add the ginger. Roll out on bread board to one-half inch thickness and cut in squares. Turn every day for a week, then put in cheese cloth bag and hang up for a week in a dry place. Put away in fruit jars.

From the 1960s back, a surprising number of church cookbooks included recipes for foods made with Grape Nuts. Had the cereal company given out recipe leaflets or printed recipes on boxes at one time? There were Grape Nut Bread, Grape Nut Pie, Grape Nut Custard, Grape Nut Plum Pudding, even directions for making Grape Nuts!

Grapenuts

1 cup buttermilk
1 egg
1 cup syrup
3 cups graham flour
1 tsp salt
1 tsp soda dissolved in milk

Mix well and bake in loaf pan in slow oven. Break in pieces, let stand until cool. Cut through food chopper and return to oven to dry and brown even. Must stir often.

Grape—Nut Bread

1 cup Grape Nuts cereal
2 cups sour milk
3 eggs
1 tsp salt
1½ cup sugar
4 cups flour
1 tsp soda

Let milk stand over grape nuts about 2 hours. Add beaten eggs, sugar, salt, flour and soda. Bake in slow oven (325°) about 1 hour.

Grape Nut Pie

½ cup grape nuts
½ cup warm water
3 eggs, beaten
¾ cup sugar
1 cup dark corn syrup
⅛ tsp salt
1 tsp vanilla
3 T melted butter

Combine grape nuts and water. Let stand until water is absorbed. Combine eggs and sugar; add syrup, vanilla and butter. Fold in softened grape nuts. Pour into unbaked pie shell. Bake at 350° for 50 minutes or until filling is puffed completely across the top. Cool and serve with whipped cream.

Grape Nut Raisin Pie

¾ cup grape-nuts
¾ cup chopped raisins
1½ cups brown sugar
2¼ cups hot water
¼ cup cider vinegar
3 T butter

Combine grape-nuts, raisins, sugar, water, vinegar and butter. Cook 10 minutes and cool. Place in unbaked pie shell and make a lattice top of strips of pastry. Bake in hot oven 425° to start and then finish baking at 350° until browned.

Grape Nuts Plum Pudding

Chill:
  2 cups boiling water
  1 pkg lemon jello
dash of salt
¾ cup walnuts
¾ cup grape-nuts
Chop:
  ¾ cup prunes
  ¾ cup raisins
  ½ tsp cinnamon
  ¼ tsp cloves

Main Dishes

Main Dishes

For the most part these are meat-based one-dish meals. We have not included ways of preparing most basic meats — roasts, baked chicken, steamed fish — but rather the ways these cooks used these meats and made the dishes unique in their time. Most are aimed at stretching meat protein with vegetables and other basics. Some are simply meant to taste wonderful!

Meat Balls

1½ lbs pork
½ lb beef
2 large potatoes, mashed
2 eggs
1 cup water
1½ cup bread or cracker crumbs
1½ cup milk
1 onion, minced
1 green pepper, minced
1 cup cream

Grind meat, add other ingredients and salt and pepper. Green pepper is optional. Mix very well. Roll into oblong cakes, roll in flour, fry in butter until brown. Add 1 cup water and bake 1 hour. Last half hour, add the cup of cream

Apple Sauce Meat Balls

Mix together well:
¾ lb ground beef
¼ lb ground pork
½ cup thick unsweetened applesauce
½ cup soft bread crumbs
1 egg, well beaten
¼ cup minced onion
1¼ tsp salt
⅛ tsp pepper

Form into 12 balls. Roll lightly in flour. Brown in small amount of hot fat in skillet. Place in baking dish or dutch oven. Over the meat balls, pour a mixture of ¼ cup catsup and ¼ cup water. Cover and bake 1¼ hours in moderate oven.

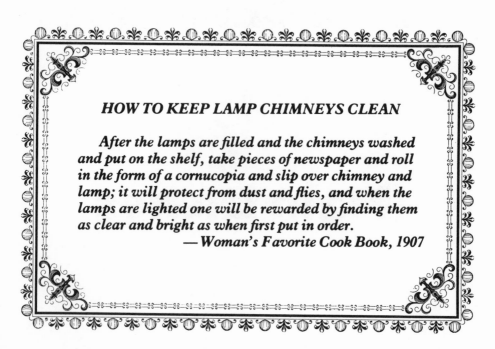

HOW TO KEEP LAMP CHIMNEYS CLEAN

After the lamps are filled and the chimneys washed and put on the shelf, take pieces of newspaper and roll in the form of a cornucopia and slip over chimney and lamp; it will protect from dust and flies, and when the lamps are lighted one will be rewarded by finding them as clear and bright as when first put in order.
— Woman's Favorite Cook Book, 1907

The DEXTER "TWIN TUB" GIVES YOU MORE TIME FOR PLAY

Want to do your washing quicker—better—
easier? Then the Dexter Twin Tub is for
you! Both tubs wash together—
get clothes twice as clean—twice as fast.
Yes, in only *60 minutes* or less you can
easily do the entire weekly washing. Come
in today and see this Modern Dexter Washer.

THE DEXTER CO.
FAIRFIELD, IOWA

The 1930s produced a "variety" meatball that still shows up in present-day books. Variously called Porcupines, Snow Balls, Snow Birds and Hamburger Hedgehogs, they call for uncooked rice that swells out from the meatballs as they simmer in diluted tomato soup. You may want to bake or cook them in a stock of your own choosing. There was even a "Porcupine Cookie" in one book; chopped nuts made a rough surface.

Porcupines

1 lb ground beef
½ lb ground lean pork
1 small onion, minced
½ cup uncooked rice (washed thoroughly)
½ cup cracker crumbs
1 egg
salt
pepper

Mix well and shape into balls and pile in oiled casserole. Pour over 1 can tomato soup or tomato sauce diluted with a little water. Bake 1 hour in moderate oven.

Snow Balls

1½ lbs shoulder pork, ground
1 cup rice, washed but not cooked

Season with salt, pepper and onion. Combine meat and rice and mold into firm balls. Dilute 1 can of tomato soup with 2 cups of water and simmer balls 1½ hours in this liquid.

Swiss Meat Loaf

2 lbs hamburger
1½ cups diced Swiss cheese
2 beaten eggs
½ cup chopped onion
½ cup chopped green pepper
1½ tsp salt
½ tsp pepper
1 tsp celery salt
½ tsp paprika
1½ cup milk
1 cup bread crumbs

Mix together in order given above. Press into a 9-5" greased loaf pan. Bake, uncovered, at 350° for 1½ hours. Serves 8.

Hotdish

(Pronounced "hot-tish," almost as in "Scottish" or "schotische.")

Garrison Keillor once observed that when Lutheran women reach heaven they think they are in church and immediately look for the basement stairs to find the kitchen.

Naturally. For they are carrying a hot dish.

From the beginning of cookbook history, church cookbooks have included recipes for macaroni, meat and tomatoes. In the late 30s the classic hot dish added a new staple: mushroom soup. There are other casseroles that serve as main dishes, but the one that occurs over and over is listed as "Favorite Hot Dish" or "EZ Casserole" or "Mom's Supper Dish" or, usually, "Hamburger Hot Dish."

You don't need a recipe. All you need are your choices of:

Meat: Browned ground beef, ground pork, ground veal, beef stew meat, chopped leftover roast, fried and crumbled bacon, ground or chopped ham. No chicken or fish for this.

With the meat you may brown chopped onions, green pepper, red pepper, celery and, if you are daring, minced garlic.

Tomatoes — canned, pureed, sauce, soup or paste.

Pasta of almost any size or shape except the wide lasagna noodles and the big ones you stuff. Or rice. Or potatoes.

To this you may add, if you wish, mushrooms, pimento, peas, broccoli, corn, carrots, zucchini, frozen mixed vegetables — or none at all.

And soup: cream of mushroom, cream of chicken, cream of celery, cream of asparagus, cream of almost anything.

Canned soups are salty so season with pepper, basil, oregano or your favorite herb.

Just before baking top with bread crumbs, cracker crumbs, crushed cereal flakes, crushed potato chips, crushed taco snacks, and/or cheese.

Choices and combinations vary with every cook. These are tasty, nourishing, fix-ahead dishes that generally appeal to both grownups and kids. While you are experimenting with various combinations, here are some other main-dish casseroles that busy women have been setting on their tables when they weren't carrying them to the church basement—or to heaven:

(A word of caution: There is such a thing as hot dish overkill. Don't be like the man who loved to bake bread and started adding all kinds of tasty nutrients—rye flour, barley flour, rice flour, wheat germ, yogurt, pine nuts, sunflower seeds, oatmeal, raisins, chopped figs, bean curd. One day the bread refused to rise. It had simply reached its limit.)

Meat Saving Casserole

1 8-oz pkg macaroni
3 T butter
¼ lb dried beef
¼ cup green pepper
3 T flour
1½ cup milk
¾ cup grated cheese
Salt and pepper

Cook macaroni in boiling water. Drain. Frizzle meat and green pepper in butter. Stir in flour and mix until smooth. Add milk and cook until thickened. Stir constantly. Add cheese, stir until melted. Season to taste. Pour this sauce over macaroni in buttered baking dish. Cover top with buttered crumbs and bake in moderate oven (350°) for 30 or 40 minutes.

Hungarian Goulash

4 lb veal shoulder cut in 2" cubes

Brown in 6 T fat; brown 1 large onion, size of your fist; add paprika, salt and pepper, 2 large fresh tomatoes, 1 cup water and boil slowly until tender. Thicken with 2 T flour and add 1 pt sweet cream. Cook potatoes as needed in plain water and add just before taking up meat.

Hot Dish

In 1 cup hot milk, soak 2½ slices fresh bread. Add 1 cup milk. Beat 4 egg yolks slightly. Add 1 cup cooked carrots and celery chopped fine (shred carrots). Must be cold before added.

Add ¼ cup or ½ cube melted butter, salt and pepper. Beat egg whites stiff. Fold into mixture. Pour in ring mold which has been oiled. Set in pan of hot water and bake in moderate oven 45 minutes. Put creamed chipped beef in center.

Spam made its appearance during World War II, a staple in c-rations, as any ex-GI can tell you. (They had other names for it.) But at home it had a big impact. At a time when "home freezer" was a tiny cubicle inside the refrigerator, here was meat that could be stored indefinitely on a cupboard shelf, ready for all kinds of emergencies. All over the country, cooks rose to the challenge.

Spam and Noodle Hot Dish

½ lb fine noodles (4 cups uncooked)*
1 can Spam, cubed
1 medium onion, chopped
2 cups chopped celery
1 small can pimento, drained and chopped (optional)
1 can cream of chicken soup
1 can cream of mushroom soup
1½ soup cans of water

Mix all ingredients; *don't add any salt* as soup and Spam are salty. Bake in a greased 2 quart casserole at 375° for 1 hour. About 5 minutes before removing from oven sprinkle 1 cup grated cheese over top and return to oven. Serves 8-10.
*Cook in unsalted water.

Spam and Asparagus Casserole

1 can Spam, cubed (½ lb shrimp may be used)
3 hard cooked eggs, sliced
2 cans asparagus (or fresh cut in 1" pieces)
1 cup grated sharp cheese
1 cup mayonnaise
1 cup melted butter
2 cups fresh bread cubes
2 cups thick white sauce
bread crumbs for topping

Put bread cubes in bottom of 13×9" pan. Cover with half of cheese and butter. Cover with layer of Spam, eggs and asparagus, using all of each. Cover with white sauce to which mayonnaise has been added. Put remaining cheese on top and cover with bread crumbs and remaining butter. Bake at 325° for 45 minutes. Serves 8-10.

Aunt Martha's Spam and Rice Casserole

1 cup uncooked rice
3 cups milk
1 tsp salt
dash pepper
1 tsp grated onion
½ shredded green pepper
1 can cream of celery soup
1 cup shredded cheese
1 cup grated carrots
1 can shredded Spam

Combine ingredients in a covered casserole and bake covered at 375 for ¾ hour or until it bgins to cook. Turn low and bake uncovered ¾ hour, or until done. Makes a good picnic dish as it holds the heat very well.

Green Rice

3 cups cooked rice
2 eggs, beaten
¾ cup milk
2 T onion
2 T parsley
2 T green pepper
Salt
Pepper

Saute onion, parsley, green pepper in butter. Mix together all ingredients. Bake at 350 about 30 minutes, or until set so knife comes out clean. Cut in squares and top with sauce. 6 to 8 servings.

Sauce: 1 can cream of mushroom soup, 1 can shrimp, crab or tuna fish; one cup sharp cheese.

6 Layer Dinner

2 cups sliced raw potatoes
2 cups sliced raw carrots
½ cup sliced onions
1 cup chopped celery
2 cups raw hamburger
2 tsp salt
¼ tsp pepper
1 can tomato soup

Place in buttered casserole in order given. Bake 1 hour at 350 to 375°.

Beef Stroganoff reached the church cookbooks in the early 1960s.

Beef Stroganoff

2½ lbs round or flank steak
4 T red wine
1 cup baby onions
½ cup sour cream
½ lb mushrooms
1 tsp catsup
2 T flour
2 cups hot water
2 bouillion cubes

Cut steak into thin crosswise strips; brown well; place in casserole; add wine. Cook onion until soft; add mushrooms thickly sliced. Cook 5 minutes. Add catsup, flour, and meat mixture; add seasonings to taste. Replace beef in pan. Cover and cook slowly until meat is tender — about 1 hour.

Just before serving, add the sour cream slowly.

Hamburger Stroganoff

½ cup minced onions
¼ cup butter or margarine
1 lb ground beef
1 clove garlic, minced (optional)
2 T flour
2 tsp salt
¼ tsp monosodium glutamate
¼ tsp pepper
¼ tsp paprika
1 lb sliced mushrooms
1 can cream of chicken soup, undiluted
1 cup sour cream
Snipped parsley, chives or fresh dill

Saute onion in butter till golden. Stir in beef and next seven ingredients, saute 5 minutes. Add soup; simmer uncovered 10 minutes. Stir in sour cream; sprinkle with parsley. Serve on hot mashed potatoes, fluffy rice, noodles or toast. Serves 4 to 6.

5-Hour Stew

2 lbs. stew meat or round steak, cubed
2 onions, sliced
1 cup celery, sliced
4-5 carrots, sliced
4 large potatoes
2 T tapioca
1 T sugar
2 tsp salt
¼ tsp pepper
1 can tomato soup
½ soupcan water

Layer ingredients in order in a deep casserole. Cover tightly and bake at 325° for 5 hours.

Tapioca Ham Loaf

½ cup minute tapioca, uncooked
1 lb lean ham, ground
1 lb lean pork, ground
1 T onion pulp
1 tsp Worcestershire sauce
¼ tsp pepper
½ tsp paprika
2 cups milk

Combine ingredients in order named and mix well. Bake in a loaf pan in hot oven, 450°. Bake 45 minutes. Serve hot or cold. Serves 10.

Baked Pork Chops

6 rib or loin chops 1" thick
1 T flour
1 1½-oz pkg dehydrated onion soup mix
2½ cups boiling water
1 cup dairy sour cream
Celery leaves or parsley

Brown chops in skillet. Remove to baking dish. Pour fat from skillet, leaving about 1 T in pan. Add flour and onion soup mix. Blend in water. Pour over chops. Cover with foil and bake 30 minutes at 350°. Uncover and bake 30–40 minutes longer. Remove and place on serving dish and garnish with celery leaves. Make gravy: Blend sour cream into liquid in pan and heat. Serves 6.

Baked Beans

2 cups navy beans
½ tsp baking soda
¼ lb salt pork or fresh side pork
1 onion
½ tsp dry mustard
⅓ tsp pepper
¼ cup molasses

Pick over beans and wash, then soak in 1 gallon of soft cold water. Let stand over night. In the morning drain, cover with fresh cold water and boil slowly until the skin breaks on the beans if you blow on them. then add ½ tsp soda and simmer a minute longer, then drain and blanch with cold water. Put beans into a bean pot, bury the pork in these, add mustard, pepper, and molasses and onion. Cover with boiling water and bake 6 to 7 hours in a slow oven. 300° F. Add more water as needed. Serves 6 to 8 people.

Pork Apples

1½ cups cold chopped pork
4 medium sized apples
1 T butter
½ tsp salt
⅛ tsp pepper

Core apples and scoop out centers. Fill centers with chopped pork and a small amount of chopped apple. Season with salt and pepper. On top of each apple place a piece of butter. Bake for thirty minutes in a moderate oven, basting from time to time. Serve with a small spoonful of sour cream and a dash of allspice.

Do-Ahead Dried Beef Casserole

1 cup milk
1 cup cream of mushroom soup
1 cup cheddar cheese, cut fine
1 cup uncooked elbow macaroni
Chopped onion to taste
1 pkg dried slice beef broken into
    bite-size pieces
2 hard boiled eggs, chopped

Stir soup until creamy with milk. Add cheese, onion, uncooked macaroni and dried beef. Fold in egg. Turn into buttered 1½ quart casserole. Refrigerate 3-4 hours or overnight.

Bake at 350°, uncovered, for 1 hour. Chicken or ham bits are good instead of dried beef. Serves 4-6.

Corned Beef Casserole

1 pkg (7 oz) macaroni, cooked and
    drained
1 can corned beef, chopped
1 can cream of chicken soup
1 cup milk
¼ to 1 cup grated American cheese
⅓ to ½ cup chopped onion
¾ cup buttered bread crumbs

Mix all ingredients together and put into buttered 1½ quart casserole. Cover with buttered crumbs and bake 1 hour in moderate oven 350°. Serves from 6 to 10. Mrs. Isaacs adds 1 can cream of mushroom soup.

Scalloped Chicken

1 medium sized stewing chicken, 4 or 5
    lbs (cooked, boned, cut up)
2 cups soft bread crumbs
1 cup cooked drained rice
¼ diced pimento
3 cups chicken stock
4 beaten eggs
1 tsp salt and pepper
¼ cup chicken fat or melted butter.

Bake in slow oven 325°. 1¼ hours. Serve with mushroom sauce:

1 lb mushrooms
4 T butter
5 T flour
2 cups chicken stock
Salt and pepper
1 T chopped parsley
1 tsp lemon

Let there be light

The coming of Rural Electrification to the farms of America in the late 1930s was a boon to country churches as well as to country people. But there was considerable opposition from private power companies. So the Rural Electric Cooperative Association was debated in churches as well as in other places.

"Preachers here," recalled one Midwesterner, "usually have three or four congregations and they run out of texts. They preached on whether God wanted farmers to have electricity. They found support for it in Genesis; 'Let there be light.' "

For the farm woman it was a breakthrough, a relief from a cycle of work and drudgery. Refrigerators, electric irons, electric washers, electric stoves, vacuum cleaners — these were far more important to her than even the flood of light that blazed from bulbs when the line along the family farm was energized.

The National Rural Electric Cooperative Association recently assembled hundreds of accounts of what happened when the lights began coming on. Among them:

One woman, after getting lights in her home, told the co-op manager, "The REA lights are a wonderful thing. Before lights, Pa was up and out in the morning and came in the house after dark. Now it takes some getting used to, but it's a wonderful thing to see what Pa really looks like in a good light."

In North Carolina, a farm wife recalled the first time she used her new electric iron. She plugged it in, patiently waited until it was properly hot, then unplugged it and ironed away until it was time to plug it in to reheat it.

In Missouri a woman ignored the flood of light as the bulbs suddenly burst into brilliance. Instead she ran to the refrigerator in the kitchen. It had stood there for several months, idle, awaiting this memorable night. She swung open the door. When she saw that the little light inside really came on, she burst into tears of relief.

A Georgia farmer told this about the coming of REA to his farm home:

"It was spring and plowing time, but I wouldn't go to the field, wanted to wait in the house to see what happened. The wife told me I was going to wear out the pull chain before we got the lights. I guess I was afraid of the bulbs bursting. They finally came on in the late afternoon. There was plenty of light outside and the Missus says, 'Aren't you going back out?' 'No,' I says, 'I'm celebrating today. I'm gonna sit here till dark and see how supper eats with a good light.' "

Clyde Ellis, the first general manager of the National Rural Electric Cooperative Association, summed it up: "The wires which tied the houses of rural people together also seemed to untie their spirits. Beginning in the early days and growing through the years, there has been some unusual quality about the rural electrification program which has drawn people of diverse political and social views together in a common purpose. The people who work for our program feel they're working in a cause or movement or crusade which many of them can't define."

Chicken Loaf

3 cups diced cooked chicken
1 cup soft bread crumbs
2 T chopped green peppers
2 T chopped pimentos
1 T parsley
½ tsp salt
¼ tsp paprika
4 eggs
⅔ cup milk
2 T melted butter

Mix ingredients and pour into buttered loaf pan. Bake 35 minutes in moderately slow oven. Let stand 5 minutes and carefully unmold. Serve with mushroom sauce. Also good sliced cold.

Pressed Chicken

Cook a chicken until tender. Remove the bones and cut chicken in fine pieces. Season broth with salt and pepper and cook down to a pint and a half. Add the chopped chicken and mix well. Pour into pan to chill. Cut in slices for serving.

Chicken Royal

1 5-lb hen
6 eggs
1 cup Post Toasties corn flakes
½ cup chicken fat
6 T flour
1 qt milk

Cook chicken until tender. Let stand in broth until cool. Remove chicken, remove meat from bones and cut in medium sized pieces with shears. Make a white sauce of the chicken, fat, flour and milk. Hard cook the eggs. Combine chicken, sliced eggs, ½ cup post toasties and the white sauce.

Pour into baking dish and sprinkle the remaining ½ cup post toasties over top. Bake in 375° oven for 30 minutes.

Chicken Casserole

2 pkgs frozen broccoli, lightly cooked
2 cups diced cooked chicken
2 cans cream of chicken soup
½ to 1 cup mayonnaise
½ tsp lemon juice
½ tsp curry powder
½ cup shredded cheese
½ cup bread crumbs
2 T butter

Place the partly cooked broccoli in the bottom of a casserole dish and arrange it evenly on the bottom. Place pieces of cooked chicken on top and cover with soup, mayonnaise, lemon juice and curry powder, combined together.

Melt some shortening and mix bread crumbs in it; then put shredded cheese on top of this. You can bake immediately or put in the freezer for future use. Real good!

Potluck Chicken

Cook 3-lb chicken with salt, whole pepper, whole allspice, 3 stalks celery, ½ onion. When tender, remove chicken, strain broth. Remove skin and cut up chicken. In broth cook ¾ cup wild rice 30 minutes; add ¾ cup white rice, cook 20 minutes, add water as necessary. Saute 3 cups sliced mushrooms in a little butter, add to rice with 1 can cream of celery soup and 1 cup cream. Add chicken, bake in casserole 45 minutes. May put buttered crumbs on top.

Chicken Stuffing

¼ cup butter
1 onion, chopped
1 cup diced celery
1½ tsp salt
1 egg, beaten
Milk or giblet stock
1 lb loaf bread
2 T chopped parsley
1½ tsp poultry seasoning

Melt butter, add onion and celery. Fry over low heat. Cut bread into cubes, add vegetable mixture, seasoning, egg and enough liquid to moisten, mix lightly with a fork. Will stuff 1 large chicken.

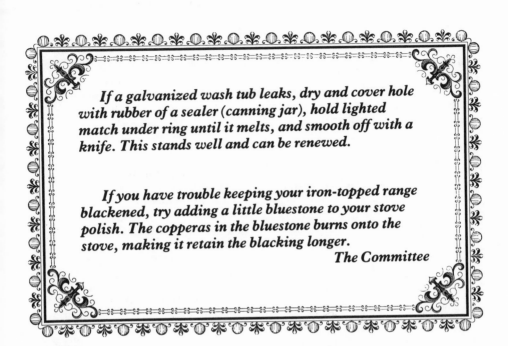

If a galvanized wash tub leaks, dry and cover hole with rubber of a sealer (canning jar), hold lighted match under ring until it melts, and smooth off with a knife. This stands well and can be renewed.

If you have trouble keeping your iron-topped range blackened, try adding a little bluestone to your stove polish. The copperas in the bluestone burns onto the stove, making it retain the blacking longer.

The Committee

Chicken Souffle

2 T flour
2 T butter
2 cups milk
½ cup bread crumbs
2 cups ground chicken
3 eggs
Parsley
2 tsp salt

Make a cream sauce of butter. flour and milk. Add salt and bread crumbs. Then add the chicken, slightly beaten egg yolks and a little parsley. Add stiffly beaten whites last. Pour in casserole. Set in pan of water and bake in moderate oven until firm.

Wild Rice Chicken Casserole

2 cans creamed chicken soup thinned
    with a little water
1 tsp salt
1 cup (raw) wild rice cooked
½ cup sliced almonds
2 cups diced chicken
¾ cup sliced mushrooms
¼ cup sliced pimento
⅓ chopped green pepper

Mix all ingredients except almonds together and pour into greased casserole. Top with sliced almonds. Bake at 350° for 1½ hours.

Chicken Divine

6 chicken breasts, boned and skinned (½
breast per serving)
2 cans cream of mushroom soup
1 cup sour cream
¼ lb dried beef
12 slices bacon
Almonds

Partially fry bacon; drain. Crumble dried beef into buttered casserole. Wrap each piece of chicken in a bacon strip. Place on dried beef. Mix soup and sour cream. Spread over chicken. Top with sliced almonds. Refrigerate, covered, overnight. Bake uncovered at 250° for 4 hours. Serve over rice, if desired. Serves 12.

When Calvary Temple in Seattle published *Heaven in the Kitchen*, it included several recipes from missionaries the church has sponsored.

Genevieve and Jim Davis are at this writing still serving in Okinawa. Gordon and Bernice Weden, who have built mission stations in Nicaragua, are now retired. Albert and Frances Brown serve in Indonesia.

Empress Chicken

1 cut-up chicken or 2½ lbs chicken parts
4 green onions cut into 1" pieces or tied
    into knots
4 slices ginger
2 T wine
5 T soy sauce
1 cup water
1 bamboo shoot sliced
2 cups mushrooms quartered
1 T sugar
1 tsp Accent

Heat 5 T oil to 400° ; fry green onions, ginger and chicken. When chicken turns white, add wine and soy sauce. Cover and cook on high heat 5-10 minutes. Turn chicken pieces and add water. Cover loosely, bring to boil, then turn to medium heat and cook 15 minutes. Add more water if necessary. After chicken has cooked for 15 minutes, add sugar, bamboo shoots, mushrooms, Accent; turn heat to low and cook about 20 minutes or until chicken is tender. Add 2 T green peas and stir for a minute or two more. This dish is good prepared ahead and reheated at serving time. Peas should be held out and added at reheating time.

—Genevieve Davis

Arroz con Pollo

2 broiler-fryer chickens
3 cups chicken broth
⅛ tsp saffron
1 tsp paprika
½ tsp pepper
1 tsp garlic salt
2 tsp salt
1 medium onion, chopped
1 bay leaf, crumbled
1½ cup uncooked rice
1 7-oz can pimento, drain & chop
2 4-oz cans mushrooms, drained and
    sliced

1 cup cooked frozen green peas
½ cup sliced stuffed olives
1 T parsley, snipped
A few capers may be added

Boil chicken until done. Remove from broth. Skin and bone, reserving chicken. In 3 cups of broth dissolve saffron, paprika, pepper, garlic salt and salt. Stir in onion and bay leaf. Add rice and cook slowly until rice is tender and dry. Mix all remaining ingredients and rice together. Serve piping hot. Serves 8.

—Bernice Widen

Peppery String Beans with Chicken Livers (Sambal Goreng ati Sama Buoontjes)

1 lb string beans
1 small onion
3 chicken livers
½ tsp tumeric
¼ tsp ground cloves
1 tsp brown sugar
1 crushed red chili
1 tsp salt, or less
½ tsp lemon peel
Little shrimp paste, if you can get it
¼ cup coconut milk (can substitute
canned milk)
2 T water
1 T butter or margarine

Soften shrimp paste. Slice beans in half. Chop onion fine. Slice livers into slivers. Saute chicken livers with onion, stir frequently. Add cloves, turmeric, brown sugar, chili, salt and lemon peel. Saute 2 minutes. Add string beans. Add milk, mix thoroughly and add shrimp paste. Cover and cook on low heat until tender. (Cut stringbeans in small pieces.)

—Frances Brown

Dayton's Skyroom Hot Dish

1 cup celery, chopped
1 medium size can mushrooms
½ cup chopped onion
3 hardboiled eggs, cut in pieces
12 stuffed olives, chopped
1 cup sharp cheese
Noodles

Make a white sauce. Blend in grated cheese. Brown celery, mushrooms and chopped onion in butter. Add all ingredients to white sauce. Serve on noodles or mix with noodles and bake until lightly browned on top.

Nigerian Curry

To make curry sauce:
1½ lb lean, tender beef or chicken, cut
　　into serving pieces
½ cup cooking oil
½ cup chopped onion
Pepper to taste
2 T curry powder (or to taste)
6 T flour
4 cups milk
2 tsp salt

Brown onion in oil, together with salted, floured cubes of meat or chicken. When thoroughly browned, remove meat and set aside. To remaining oil (add more if needed), blend in flour and curry powder. When smooth, stir in milk until thickened. Season with salt and pepper. Add meat to sauce and simmer slowly about two hours. Stir occasionally, adding small amount of milk if sauce gets too thick. (For quicker preparation, cook meat ahead of time, add the sauce and simmer for short time to let flavors blend).

　　Serve above with fluffy rice, allowing ⅔ cup rice per person. Sprinkle a small amount of any or all of these condiments over the curry and rice: diced pineapple, diced bananas, orange segments, chopped tomatoes, shredded coconut, peanuts, whole or chopped, chopped onions, diced cantaloupe, chutney.

　　If desired, top all with ground red pepper or sprinkling of hot sauce. Serves 4-5.

Alaska Lunch

Raw potatoes
Flaked salmon or tuna
2 cups cooked corn or peas
Grated raw carrots
Chopped onion
2 T melted butter
Juice from fish plus enough milk to make
　　2 cups

Butter a deep baking dish and add a 1-inch layer of thinly sliced raw potatoes. Add a layer of flaked tuna fish or salmon, then 2 cups of peas or corn, another layer of potatoes, and top with a cup of grated raw carrots and one finely chopped onion. Season each layer with salt and pepper as desired. Pour 2 cups fish liquid and milk over mixture and bake 45 minutes at 350°.

Spanish Main Rice

1 cup rice
1 lb hamburger
1 stalk celery
1 green pepper
1 medium onion
2 cans tomato soup and one cup water

Cook rice until partly done, about 20 minutes. Drain. Brown the hamburger. Saute the chopped vegetables. Mix these with meat, rice, soup and water. Season to taste. Dot with butter and grated cheese and bake in moderate oven one hour.

Some recipes are reminders of special occasions. This one is from Our Favorites, *Clarkfield (Minnesota) Lutheran Church Women, 1964.*

Kay's Graduation Hot Dish

1 can chunk light tuna
1 can crab meat
1 can shrimp
3 cups chopped celery
1 green pepper chopped (⅔ cup)
1 medium onion chopped
1 tsp salt
¼ tsp pepper
Paprika and Lee's Seasoning to taste
1 can mushroom soup
2 tsp lemon juice
1 cup Miracle Whip
¾ cup uncooked rice
1 cup buttered bread crumbs

Cook rice. Mix ingredients and pour into well buttered baking dish and top with bread crumbs. Bake 1 hour at 350°. Serves 12.

Salmon Loaf

1 cup flaked salmon
1 cup bread crumbs
1 cup scalded milk
1 tsp salt
1 T butter
½ tsp onion juice
2 egg yolks, beaten
1 tsp lemon juice
2 egg whites stiffly beaten

Combine ingredients in order given, having soaked bread crumbs in scalded milk. Fold in egg whites last. Place in a well greased pan and bake in a moderately hot oven or steam the mixture. Serve with white sauce.

Salmon Patties

1 cup salmon
1 egg, beaten
2 cups mashed potatoes
Salt and pepper

Form into patties, roll in crumbs and fry until nicely browned.

Harness Making Our Specialty!

FLY-NETS - COLLARS - PADS - BRIDLES, ETC.

HARNESS AND BINDER CANVAS REPAIRING

M. F. WILLIAMS

110 WEST 17TH. STREET   FALLS CITY, NEBR.

Fisherman's Casserole

1 pkg frozen mashed potatoes or 2 cups
   homemade
1 can (3-oz) mushrooms
1 can (10½-oz) cream of mushroom soup
2 cans (6½-oz) tuna
1 cup grated American cheese
1 medium onion, chopped
½ green pepper, chopped
½ tsp salt
¼ tsp pepper
3 hard-cooked eggs

Start oven at 350°. Grease 2 quart
casserole. Prepare frozen mashed potatoes
according to package directions or fluff up
some left-over ones of your own. Chop
mushrooms fine, toss in with cream of
mushroom soup and ½ cup grated cheese.
Cook over low heat until cheese melts. Add
onion, green pepper and all seasonings.
Slice hard cooked eggs and arrange a layer
over bottom of casserole, cover with a layer
of drained tuna and a layer of sauce.
Repeat the layers ending with sauce layer.
Spread mashed potatoes over surface and
sprinkle with remaining cheese. Bake 30 to
35 minutes. Serves 6.

Oyster Rarebit

Clean and remove the hard muscle from ½
pt oysters; put 1 T butter and ½ lb cheese
into the chafing dish; mix 1 saltspoon each
of salt, mustard and a dash of cayenne
pepper. While this mixture is melting beat
2 eggs and add to the oyster liquor. Mix
this gradually with the melted cheese, then
add the oysters and serve at once on hot
toast.

Hangtown Fry

3 small sausages cut crosswise in rings
1 cup oysters drained
2 eggs slightly beaten

Fry sausages until medium brown, put
oysters in with the sausage rings and when
oysters curl at the edges stir in eggs. Cook
until they are set. Stir as for scrambled
eggs. Serve with toast.

Fish Pudding

1 tall can pink salmon, cleaned
2 eggs
¾ cup canned milk
½ cup melted butter
Salt and pepper
½ tsp (after grating) *whole* ground nutmeg

Beat with electric mixer a good 30 minutes
on "high." ("Beat the life out of it!") Bake
in greased loaf pan (set in pan of water) 45
minutes in a 350 oven.

Crab Stuffed Peppers

2 cups crab meat
2 cups bread crumbs
2 cups tomato pulp
⅓ cup butter
½ tsp salt
¼ tsp pepper
2 cups water
6 medium peppers, seeded, halved

Parboil the peppers until tender, then fill
well. Sprinkle bread crumbs over top. Add
two cups water. Bake 30 minutes. Serve
with brown sauce or tomato sauce.

Hot Crab Souffle

8 slices white bread
2 cups crab or shrimp
1 green pepper, chopped
3 cups milk
1 can cream of mushroom soup
½ cup mayonnaise
1 medium onion
1 cup chopped celery
4 eggs
Grated medium sharp cheese
Paprika

Dice 4 slices bread and put in baking dish.
Mix crab, mayonnaise, onion, green
pepper and celery. Spread over diced
bread. Trim crusts from other 4 slices of
bread and place over crab mixture. Mix
milk and eggs together and pour over.
Place in refrigerator overnight. Bake at
325° for 15 minutes; take out and spoon
mushroom soup (mixed with ¼ cup milk)
over top. Sprinkle with grated cheese and
paprika. Bake 1 hour at 325°.

Marshall Auto Co. 122-24 EAST MAIN
THE MAIN ST. GARAGE
MARSHALLTOWN, IOWA
VELIE, HUPMOBILE and PREMIER SIX. A full line of Accessories and Supplies. Repair work a specialty by skilled workmen. See our line before you buy.

Fish Chowder

2 lb cod or haddock *or*
1 can flaked fish
3 cups potatoes, cut in ¼" slices *or*
2 cups potatoes cut in ¾" cubes
½ slices onion
1 cube fat salt pork (¼ lb)
1 T salt
⅛ tsp pepper
1½ T butter
2 cups scalded milk
½ box Uneeda biscuits (about 20 soda
   crackers)

Break cooked fish in small pieces. Set aside. Parboil potatoes. Cut pork in very small cubes and fry. Drain most of fat, cook onion in fry pan till golden. Mix everything together, let barely simmer for 10 minutes.

Howard's Fish Chowder

2 lbs fish, cut in ¾-inch pieces, cooked
2 cans cream of potato soup, diluted with
   water
1 can cream of celery soup, diluted with
   water
1 big handful frozen hash browns
Simmer 5-10 minutes.
Optional:
2 cans clams, with liquid
Chopped onion
Small frozen shrimp
Corn

Escalloped Oysters

1 pt oysters
1 cup grated bread crumbs
½ cup coarse cracker crumbs
⅛ tsp pepper
½ cup butter
1 cup milk
1 tsp salt

Drain and clean the oysters; line a pudding dish thickly with butter, sprinkle the bottom with bread crumbs. Mix the rest of the bread and cracker crumbs and stir in the butter. Arrange the oysters and crumbs in alternate layers, season each layer with pepper and salt. Pour over the milk, and bake 30 minutes in a quick oven.

Congratulations to the Women

of the Morrill Community upon the publication of this fine Cook Cook.

Realizing that you are making every effort to increase the production of dairy products on the farm let us call your attention to your "First Assistant" in the Dairy—the famous McCormick-Deering Stainless Steel Separator. It gets the most cream and makes the most profit for you.

"BUY WAR BONDS AND STAMPS WITH THE SAVINGS"

Falls City Implement Co.

Southeast Nebraska's Largest Farm Machinery Store

During World War II the Willing Workers Class of the Church of the Brethren in Morrill, Kansas, called on local merchants to help fund their cookbook. The Fall City Implement Company's ad congratulated the Willing Workers upon publication of the fine cookbook and highlighted their ad with a photo of a woman turning the crank of a gleaming McCormick-Deering Stainless Steel Cream Separator. "Buy War Bonds and Stamps With the Savings." Not only did the ads reflect the solid Kansas farming community — harness repairing, binder canvas repairing, buyers of poultry, eggs and cream, baby chicks ("Single Comb Reds, White Rocks, Hatches Monday and Thursday"), Hiawatha Brand Feeds, Universal Short Tube Milking Machines, fly nets, Crosley radios, Massey Harris Farm Machinery — but the book must have come out just before an election: several candidates for county office asked for support.

Bouillon

Three pounds of beef in the leg, 1 pound veal and mutton. Have all cut rather small. Put on the stove in enough water to keep from burning and let it brown. After it is browned add 3 quarts of boiling water, 5 or 6 stalks of celery, 1 carrot cut in bits, a small turnip cut up, 2 or 3 onions fried brown in a little butter or beef drippings, and 6 or 8 cloves and allspice. Put all in the kettle and let it cook 3 or 4 hours slowly, covered. Strain through a thin cloth or fine colander and set aside over night. Take the cake of fat off, then the jellied portion, leaving any sediment that may be in the bottom. Put jellied part on to heat, add 1 tablespoonful Worcestershire Sauce and 1 or 2 of catsup. After it comes to a boil strain again through a fine cloth. Serve as is or as the base for vegetable soups.

Cotton Batting Soup

For six people: One cup of flour, milk enough to stir smooth; add 3 eggs, beat thoroughly; let run into boiling beef stock and boil 2 minutes.

Split Pea Soup

2 cups dry split peas
2 cups cold water
Season to taste
1 small onion
1 qt thin white sauce
¾ cup chopped ham, if possible

Soak peas over night, drain, cook peas and onion in water slowly until very soft. Rub through sieve, add to white sauce and diced ham.

Peanut Butter Soup

2 cups scalded milk
1 T flour
1 T butter
1 tsp salt
¼ tsp pepper
2 T peanut butter
A suspicion of onion juice

Add peanut butter to hot milk and rub well to thoroughly mix. Add butter and seasonings, then butter with the flour made into a smooth paste with a little milk.

Quick Dumplings for Vegetable Soup

2 eggs beaten
½ cup water
1 tsp baking powder
1 tsp salt
1 to 1½ cups flour

Mix all together and add enough flour to form into balls with a spoon. (To keep the dumplings from sticking to the spoon, dip the spoon into soup first each time you drop another dumpling into soup.) Cook 10 minutes without a cover.

Wooden Shoes

1 cup flour
1 T shortening
¾ tsp salt
¾ cup milk
3 eggs

Put large cast-iron skillet on low heat with shortening in it. Set oven at 450. Sift flour and salt into bowl and gradually add milk, stirring until smooth. Add eggs and beat just enough to distribute yolks, but leave whites streaky. Turn up heat under skillet. Watch for first sign of smoke, then quickly pour in batter. As soon as edge crinkles, while center is still soft, turn over quickly. Pop into oven. Bake 5 minutes for custard-y center; 7 minutes for permanent pancake. Top with: confectioners sugar or maple syrup; fruit sauce. Wooden shoes are versatile. Top them with anything you like.

Brown Rice and Cheese

3 cups milk
2 eggs
2 cups boiled brown rice
2 cups grated cheese
1 tsp salt
¼ tsp paprika

Scald milk, add beaten eggs and other ingredients. Pour into buttered custard cups, set in a pan of hot water and bake in a 350 F. oven until done, that is, when a knife inserted in the center of the custard comes out clean. Pimentos, if liked are an attractive addition.

Feather-Light Waffles

3 cups sifted flour
 2 heaping tsp baking powder
1½ tsp salt
4 egg yolks
1 qt milk
½ lb butter (melted)
4 egg whites (beaten well but not dry)

Put flour, baking powder, and salt in a good sized bowl. Stir with spoon lightly. Add half the milk. Then add egg yolks and melted butter. Beat until smooth. Add rest of milk. A little more than a quart of milk can be used if necessary to make a medium thin batter. Fold in beaten egg whites. This makes 24 medium-sized waffles that are feather light.

Cream Waffles

1½ cup flour
1½ rounding tsp baking powder
1 T sugar
Salt to taste

Sift. Add to

1 cup cream (top cream will do)
3 egg yolks

Mix. Add stiffly beaten egg whites. Makes 6 waffles.

Salads

Chicken Salad for 25

The "Chicken Salad for 25" is from a book put out by the Covenant Women of the Dassel (Minnesota) Covenant Church. The recipe is signed "Charlotte Lindholm," and it instantly evokes memories of the farm where Charlotte Olson Lindholm grew up. It was a very special little farm, for if you followed the sloping pasture to the north it brought you to the shores of Little Lake.

One of the greatest adventures of winter for any child in Minnesota was being allowed to go along on the bobsled to harvet ice for the icehouse, ice that would be packed in sawdust in a special shed to last through the long hot summer.

The excursion would be in January, the coldest time of year, when the ice was thickest and it had not yet begun to soften with February's mellowing. Likely it was several degrees below zero, with that pale sun hanging in the south and the horses trumpeting steam through their great nostrils. I would be in long underwear, long stockings, buckled overshoes, "snow pants" (probably home-made from someone's old coat), sweater upon sweater, coat, wool stocking cap, two pairs of mittens and a wool scarf knotted so that little beads of frost edged it just below my steaming nose.

How deliciously scary to clop, clop, clop out to the center of the lake, to know that all that lay between us and that cold green water was this vast sheet of snow-crusted ice. Eyes closed, I would plot my escape in case a great crack suddenly split under the horses' hooves. How satisfying to find stretches of clear blue ice where blizzard winds had swept the snow to drifts on the far banks; sometimes I brought skates that clamped shakily to the soles of my overshoes. And if I was feeling particularly brave I would creep, spellbound, to the edge of the chasm where rectangles of ice bobbed in the frigid water, ready to be hauled out, cut in great cubes and loaded on the sleigh.

The trip home seemed much longer. The horses tugged more slowly at the heavy load, the sun was nearing the snowy horizon, the wind was in our faces and my toes had begun to feel numb.

It seemed fitting to me that the Dassel Covenant Women's "Recipes and Reflections" carried many recollections by various people of the church's early days. (It was founded in 1878.) Here, by permission, are some of them, along with Charlotte's wonderful Chicken Salad for 25:

"One fond memory is going to Julotta early Christmas morning when we were children. My father driving the horses with sleigh bells ringing. Mother, my brothers and myself warm and snug in the bobsled. There was hay in the bottom of the sled and blankets to keep us warm. It was usually very cold, but it was beautiful. Once we tipped over when we struck a ridge in the road. By ridge I mean a snowbank. How we laughed as we got out of the snow, brushed ourselves off somewhat and got back in the sled."

The smell of coffee just coming to a boil floats through a building like magic. The Dassel Covenant Church cook book recalls this comment spoken by a chairman of a meeting many years ago: "I think it's time to close the meeting. I can smell the ladies in the kitchen."

"Many years ago Ladies Aid was a great town event, for all the people of the town knew that there was sure to be a most delicious meal. Many working ladies would bring lunch from the Mission Church's Ladies Aid to fellow workers. The yeast plant had their lunch from there, and so forth. The ladies in the kitchen knew that they would be feeding up to 200 people lunch plus dessert (which sometimes were angel food cakes made without any electric equipment).

"One day two little girls ran home saying, 'Mommy, Mommy, we just had lunch at the Mission Church Ladies Aid and it was so good!' Later the mother found out that they got in on a funeral lunch and not ladies aid."

"Aleda Swanson remembers well the Sunday School programs. She said her long stockings always seemed to be wrinkled while Darby Spath's looked nice and smooth. She also remembers wanting to sit near the Rev. A.G. Petersons at the New Year's Wake service because Rev. Peterson always kissed his wife Fannie when the clock showed midnight. And whoever heard of kissing in church in those days?"

"The pastor's salary was very low but he was given a side of beef or eggs or garden produce by many. Also hay was bought for his horse. Mr. John Rosander's father, Mr. Adolph Erickson, usually gave a bag of oats to the pastor, but when he forgot, Rev. Sjoquist reminded him that he then owed him two bags of oats."

"Rev. Sjoquist's first salary was $200 a year. He had five children."

"When serving first began at the church, a large three-burner kerosene stove was used. On two burners were tubs of water, one for washing and one for rinsing dishes, and the third burner held the boiler used for cooking coffee. The Wreisner auto dealers always sent up a basket with a coffee pot in it, plus a dollar donation, and the ladies sent it back full of coffee and lunch for the workers at the garage.

"What a job butchering day was! Meat was cut up and sometimes salted down or put in crocks with pork fat layered over the top. However, this did not keep too long so a more popular method was that of canning the meat in good-sized chunks. Those who had meat grinders or could borrow them made meat balls in large cast iron pans on the stove, and then packed them carefully in jars, pouring the drippings on top and processing them in the oven of the big black range that presided over the kitchen. Of course countless chickens were canned. Most people had a few hens that were too old for laying, but after being procesed in the oven, they were tender and juicy and perfect for those Ladies Aid sandwiches." And for:

Chicken Salad for 25

2 good-sized chickens
4 T salad oil
4 T orange juice
4 T vinegar
2 tsp salt
2 cups mandarin orange sections
3 cups pineapple tidbits
3 cups green onions
2 cups slivered almonds, toasted
3 cups diced celery
2½ cups raw rice
1 quart mayonnaise

Cook chicken until tender. Remove meat from bones and cube. Mix together salad oil, orange juice, vinegar and salt. marinate chicken in this in the refrigerator. Then add the fruits, nuts and celery. While chicken is marinating, cook rice until tender in boiling salted water. Drain and blanch in cold water. Add drained rice to salad, toss with mayonnaise. Serves 25.

Salad Dressing

Put in mixing bowl but do not beat:
2 egg yolks
2 T vinegar
2 T lemon juice
1 cup salad oil
½ tsp sugar
1 tsp salt
½ tsp mustard
⅛ tsp paprika

Make a white sauce of 1 cup water, ⅓ cup flour and 1 T butter. Add to above while hot and beat until blended. Never fails and keeps indefinitely.

Fruit Salad Dressing

4 egg yolks, beaten
½ tsp salt
4 egg whites, beaten
1 cup powdered sugar
Juice of 2 lemons

Add the powdered sugar gradually to the egg yolks. When the sugar is dissolved add the lemon juice. Cook until thick, cool and add beaten whites. Keep in a cool place and mix with whipped cream when ready to use.

Cooked Mayonnaise

2 T flour
1½ tsp salt
½ tsp paprika
¼ tsp mustard
¼ cup vinegar
2 T oil
½ cup hot water

Cook in double boiler until smooth stirring constantly and then cook 10 minutes longer. Cool and add one egg yolk slightly beaten and gradually ½ cup of oil, then fold in stiffly beaten white of egg if desired.

Potato Salad Dressing

6 slightly beaten eggs
½ cup vinegar
⅓ cup sugar
1 tsp dry mustard
Dash of pepper
1 tsp salt
4 T butter

Mix together and cook over medium heat until thick. Thin to desired consistency with cream or top milk.

Potato Salad Dressing

1 cup sour cream
1 T corn starch
½ cup sugar
½ cup vinegar
½ tsp salt
⅛ tsp pepper
½ tsp dry mustard

Mix all very well and boil till thick, stirring constantly. Cool.

Shoestring Potato Salad

1 cup grated raw carrots
1 cup diced celery
4 hard boiled eggs, diced
½ tsp grated onion
2 cups broken Tuna
1 cup Miracle Whip
Add: 1 can (No. 2) Shoestring Potatoes

Mix all together and chill for 1 hour.

Potato Salad

Cook 7 medium potatoes in jackets. While warm, peel and slice. Pour ⅓ cup oil and vinegar dressing over potatoes. (Recipe: ½ cup oil; 2 T vinegar; 1 tsp salt; garlic and onion powder; pepper) Let stand for 2 hours.

Add:

4 hard cooked eggs, sliced (You may reserve a yolk to sieve over top for garnish.)
⅓ cup green onions and tops, sliced
1 cup mayonnaise
½ cup cultured cream, sour
2 tsp dill weed
¾ cup diced celery

Chill.

German Potato Salad

Wash and boil 4 potatoes. While hot, peel and slice thin with 1 small, raw onion. Sprinkle with salt and pepper. Put a T of butter in a spider. Let it brown, pour in ⅔ cup of vinegar. When it boils up pour it over the salad. Add 2 sliced hard boiled eggs.

Potato Salad For 100

25 lbs potatoes, cooked & sliced
12 T salt
1 T pepper
3 dozen eggs, boiled hard and chopped
2½ qts salad dressing
½ pt cream
7 qts celery, ground
¾ qt onions, ground
1 T mustard
¼ cup vinegar

Mix potatoes, chopped eggs, celery and onions. Blend together salad dressing, cream, vinegar, mustard, salt and pepper. Mix with potato mixture. Makes 3 square plastic dishpans full.

German Cabbage Salad

6 slices of bacon, diced
2 cups of shredded cabbage
1 small onion
4 T sugar
Salt and pepper
¼ cup vinegar

Shred cabbage, sprinkle a little salt over it and let stand. Brown bacon in hot pan, then remove bacon. Into the hot bacon grease pour vinegar, sugar, a little pepper, and place on stove, stirring ingredients until the sugar is dissolved. Pour over the cabbage, tossing lightly with a fork. Sprinkle bacon over the top, and serve at once. This is also good on buttered beans and shredded lettuce. Dilute the vinegar with a little water if very strong.

Norwegian Slaw For a Crowd

Toss 3 heads cabbage, chopped fine, with 1 T salt; let stand for 3 hours. Squeeze out water, add 1 green pepper, 1 small bunch celery, chopped, plus 1 onion, chopped fine. Boil together for 5 minutes; 4 cups sugar, 2 cups vinegar, 1 cup water, 1 T celery seed, 1 T mustard seed. Let cool, then pour over cabbage and let stand for 24 hours before serving. Will keep for 2 months.

Uncooked Dressing for Cabbage

1 egg
½ cup vinegar
2 T sour cream
2 T sugar
Salt and pepper

Mix above ingredients. Butter may be substituted for cream. Pour over cold or hot cabbage.

Old Fashioned Cole Slaw

1 pkg lemon flavored gelatin
½ tsp salt
1 cup hot water
½ cup cold water
½ cup mayonnaise
1 tsp sugar
½ cup cultured sour cream
1 T prepared mustard
2 T vinegar
2 cups finely shredded cabbage

Dissolve gelatin and salt in hot water. Add cold water and chill until just syrupy. Then fold in remaining ingredients except cabbage. Chill until slightly thickened. Fold in cabbage. Chill until firm.

Wilted Lettuce

Place in a vegetable dish tender lettuce that has been carefully washed and drained. Cut a slice of bacon into dice and fry until brown; when very hot add ½ cup of vinegar and pour it boiling hot over the lettuce; mix well with a fork and garnish with hard boiled eggs.

Lima Bean Salad

Combine lima beans, chopped pickled beets, tomatoes, chopped celery, peas and onions. Mix with mayonnaise. Cool and serve on crisp lettuce.

Beet Salad

1 can diced beets
2 T vinegar
2 pkg lemon jello
1 T horseradish
3½ cups beet juice and water (hot)
1 cup diced cheese
½ tsp celery salt
2 tsp salt
2 tsp grated onion

Cool slightly before adding beets and cheese. Serves 8 or 10.

Confetti Salad

1 envelope gelatin
½ cup cold water
½ cup cream
1 cup Miracle Whip
½ cup chopped green pepper
½ cup chopped pimento
1 cup chopped celery
¼ tsp chopped onion
¾ tsp salt

Soften gelatin in cold water. Dissolve over hot water and cool a little. Slowly add cream to Miracle Whip. Beat until stiff. Add gelatin and beat again. Add all above ingredients and pour into molds.

Chicken Salad

4 cups diced chicken
6 hard boiled eggs
1 cup celery, diced small
½ green pepper, diced
2 T diced pimento
1 pt whipped cream
¾ cup homemade dressing
½ cup Miracle Whip

Season to taste with salt and paprika.

Christmas Salad

Dissolve one package lemon jello in one cup boiling water. Add 3 oz cream cheese and 16 cut up marshmallows. Stir until dissolved. Refrigrate until beginning to set. Add one small can crushed pineapple and juice, 1 cup mayonnaise, and 1 cup cream, whipped. Put between layers of red and green jello in mold or pan.

Frothy Salad

1 pkg lime jello
1 cup boiling water
1 3-oz pkg cream cheese
1 can crushed pineapple, with juice
½ cup chopped celery
½ cup chopped cucumber
½ cup chopped nuts
4 T sugar
1 tsp vanilla
1 cup heavy cream whipped
Lettuce
Cherries

Dissolve gelatin in boiling water. Soften cream cheese; add hot gelatin mixture. Beat with electric mixer or egg beater until smooth. Add pineapple and juice, cool, add celery, cucumber and nuts, mix lightly. Add sugar and vanilla to whipped cream and fold into gelatin mixture. Pour into a dampened mold and chill until firm. Unmold on lettuce and top with cherries. Serves 6 to 10.

Reception Salad

1 pkg lemon jello
1 large can crushed pineapple (drained)
2 pkg cream cheese, mashed with 1 small can pimento
½ cup celery (cut fine)
½ pt cream, whipped
⅛ tsp salt

Mix lemon jello with pineapple juice which has been boiled. When it is cool and begins to jell, add other ingredients in order given. Pour into individual molds and set.

Cottage Cheese Ring

1 pkg lime jello
1 cup boiling water
¼ cup lemon juice
¼ tsp salt
¼ tsp dry mustard
⅓ cup dry milk

Mix together and let set until firm. Beat with mixer for 5 minutes until light and fluffy. Fold in:

¼ cup dairy sour cream
¼ cup green pepper
1 cup celery
1 tsp onion

Place in ring mold. Dissolve:

1 pkg lime jello
1 cup boiling water
1 cup undrained crushed pineapple

When partially set, put on top of first mixture in ring mold. Serve with cottage cheese.

Lime Jello Salad

1 pkg lime jello
¾ cup hot water
1 cup crushed pineapple
⅓ cup sugar
1 cup cottage cheese
1 cup cream, whipped
Nut meats and cherries (if desired)

Dissolve jello and sugar in hot water. Cool, add pineapple, cottage cheese, whipped cream, nuts and cherries. Pour in mold until set.

Ginger Ale Salad

1 pkg lime jello
1 cup boiling water
1 cup ginger ale
½ cup nut meats (chopped)
½ cup green cherries
½ cup red cherries
½ cup grated pineapple (drained)

Dissolve the jello in boiling water. Cool and add the ginger ale. Chill until it begins to congeal and add the fruit and nuts. Mold and chill.

Frozen Marshmallow Pineapple Salad

Combine about 32 marshmallows (quartered) with 1 cup crushed pineapple, ¼ cup pimento or American cheese, grated, and ¼ cup mayonnaise. Fold in ½ cup heavy cream, whipped. Pour in refrigerator tray and freeze. Cut and serve on lettuce leaf. Top with maraschino cherry. Serve with mayonnaise. Serves six or seven.

Five and One Salad

1 cup pineapple tidbits
1 cup mandarin oranges
1 cup marshamllow bits
1 cup flaked coconut
1 cup sour cream

Mix all together. Let mellow four or five hours, or overnight.

Cinnamon Applesauce Salad

1 T red cinnamon candies
1 cup hot water
1 pkg cherry flavored gelatin
2 cups sweetened applesauce
½ cup chopped celery
½ cup chopped nuts

Melt candies in hot water, if necessary heat till dissolved. Pour over gelatin, stirring to dissolve. Add applesauce and chill till partially set. Fold in celery and nuts. Chill till firm.

Cranberry Salad

2 lbs (6 cups) raw cranberries
2 oranges
2 cups white sugar
1 lb marshmallows
1 cup celery, cut fine
1 cup nut meats, chopped
1 pt cream (whipped)
1 tsp vanilla

Grind the cranberries and oranges; cover with sugar and let stand. Combine with rest of ingredients and refrigerate for several hours.

Cranberry Salad

1 qt cranberries
1½ cup diced celery or apples
1 cup cold water
Salt
2 T gelatin
2 cups sugar
1 cup nuts

Wash cranberries, cover with 1 cup cold water, cook until tender about three minutes, add sugar, cook 5 minutes more, soften gelatin in ⅓ cup cold water, add gelatin and salt to cranberries, stir until dissolved. Chill until thick, add celery and nuts, put in mold and chill.

Twelve Hour Salad

2 eggs beaten
5 T lemon juice
5 T sugar
2 T butter
2 cups diced pineapple
½ lb cut marshmallows
¼ lb blanched almonds or other nuts
1 cup cream
2 cups white cherries, cut in halves

Put eggs in double boiler, add sugar and lemon juice, beating constantly. Remove from fire, add butter and marshamllows and cool. When cold, fold in whipped cream and fruit mixtures. Salad should be made 12 hours in advance and stored in refrigerator. Unmold and serve on lettuce leaf. Serves 10.

Fruit Salad Dressing

1 cup of pineapple juice or juice from
   fruit cocktail
Add juice of 1 lemon
Juice of 1 orange
¼ tsp salt
½ cup sugar
2 beaten eggs or 4 to 6 yolks
1 tsp cornstarch

Mix salt, sugar, eggs and cornstarch with
enough juice or water to mix well.
Combine fruit juices in double boiler and
bring to boiling point. Add cornstarch
mixture and cook until the thickness of a
heavy cream sauce. This can be kept in
cold place in glass jar indefinitely. For
serving, it can be used this way or it can be
combined with whipped cream.

Candlestick Salad

1 slice pineapple
⅓ red cherry
½ banana
Mayonnaise dressing

Place a whole slice of pineapple on a salad
plate. Cut a straight banana in half
crosswise. Stand half of the banana in
upright position in center of pineapple
slice. Make a cut in the top of banana and
insert cherry for a flame. Serve with
dressing.

Cherry Coke Salad

1 #2 can sour cherries
1 cup water
½ cup sugar
2 boxes cherry Jello
1 #2 can crushed pineapple, drained and
   chilled
1 bottle CocaCola, chilled
1 cup nut meats (optional)

Mix the cherries, juice, water and sugar
and boil a few minutes. Pour over Jello and
stir well. Cool. Add chilled pineapple,
Coke and nuts. Refrigerate. This can be
made the day before serving and serves 10
generously.

*The abundance of dressings for vegetable
salads probably blossomed in the 1950s and
continued to multiply. And while you
probably can't do better than some olive oil,
flavored vinegar and your favorite herbs or
mustards, here are two:*

Blue Cheese Dressing

2 cups mayonnaise
1 cup sour half and half
1 9-oz can condensed milk
2 cloves garlic, minced
2 tsp lemon juice
2 tsp sugar
2-3 drops hot sauce or dash of cayenne

Beat well and add 2 or more ounces of blue
cheese.

French Dressing

1 small can tomato sauce
1 can tomato soup
1 onion, chopped fine
¾ cup sugar
¾ cup cider vinegar
1 tsp dried basil
½ tsp dry mustard
½ tsp paprika
1 cup vegetable oil
¼ cup olive oil
1 tsp salt (optional)

Beat well and store in tight container in
refrigerator. If you like a sweeter dressing
increase sugar to one cup.

Tapioca Pudding Fruit Salad

1 pkg Jello orange pudding
1 pkg Jello vanilla tapioca pudding
2 cans mandarin oranges
1 large or 2 small cans pineapple tidbits

Drain cans of fruit and save liquid, take 3
cups of the liquid (fill with water if not
enough), and stir it into pudding and bring
to boil, remove from heat and let cool. It
thickens as it cools. When cool, add fruit.
(Pineapple, oranges, bananas, apples,
grapes may be used if desired.)

Fruit Salad Dressing

2 egg whites
2 egg yolks
½ cup sugar
Juice of 1 lemon
Whipped cream

Beat yolks and whites of eggs thoroughly and add together with sugar, juice of lemon. Cook over hot water until thick. When cold and ready to use, thin with whipped cream.

Fruit Salad

Mix 7 T sugar, 2 T flour, 2 beaten eggs, scant teaspoon prepared mustard, and juice from 1 #2 can pineapple chunks. Cook until it thickens. Add a chunk of butter and cool. When ready to serve, add pineapple, 4 bananas, 1 dozen marshmallows, and 1 small bottle red maraschino cherries.

Retired pastor Paul Seastrand of Lindstrom, Minnesota, growing up in a country parish at Knapp, north of Cokato, Minnesota, depended on summer work at nearby farms to provide a little income for high school.

"That one summer, classes over until fall, I reported for work at eight a.m. at the Smedberg farm."

Mrs. Smedberg, a chipper little woman, had, since her husband's death several years earlier, run the farm with the help of her son and schoolteacher daughter.

"My first assignment was to hoe thistles in the corn field at the south end of the farm. It was beyond a hill and I was out of sight of the farm buildings.

"As on most farms, there was 'forenoon lunch' at ten and 'afternoon lunch' at three. Mrs. Smedberg put a pint jar full of coffee, some cookies and doughnuts in a tin pail, the kind Karo syrup came in.

"Then she called Rex, as lovely a little fox terrier as you'd ever see. She put the wire handle of the pail in his mouth and, pointing in my direction, said, 'Rex, go bring this lunch to Paul.'

"Rex would take off at once. How did he know in what part of the field to find me? For there he would be, letting go of the handle only when I took it from him. And the look on his face when I took that first bite of cookie and first sip of coffee! It would have melted the heart of any farm hand, and of course we shared that pail of goodies.

"Rex was later run over by a car and killed. If there is such a thing as a 'dog heaven,' then Rex will most certainly be there. Saint Bernard will ask no questions as the little fox terrier goes through those Pearly Gates, wagging tail and all."

62

Vegetables

Asparagus Custard

1¾ cups asparagus
3 eggs
½ tsp grated lemon rind
2 cups milk
2½ T melted butter
Pepper and salt to taste
Dash of nutmeg (may be omitted)

Cook asparagus, which has been chopped into three-inch pieces, until tender but firm. Drain. Beat eggs with rotary beater till light. Then add all other ingredients. Pour into greased baking-dish. Set in pan of hot water and bake in moderate oven till custard is firm.

Carrot Ring

3 cups finely cut cooked carrots
1 tsp salt
½ tsp pepper
2 tsp minced onions
4 or 5 slightly beaten eggs
1½ cups milk

Mix ingredients and pour into a well greased mold. Set in a pan of hot water and bake 35 minutes or until firm. Bake in a moderate hot oven. Unmold and fill with buttered peas.

Corn Fritters

1 cup canned corn
5/8 cup flour
½ tsp baking powder
½ tsp salt
1 egg
Few grains paprika

Mix and sift dry ingredients: add corn. Add beaten egg yolk. Fold in egg whites beaten until stiff. Deep fry until delicately browned. Serve hot with butter and syrup.

Corn Fritters

One dozen ears of sweet corn grated, 3 eggs, 2 tablespoonfuls of milk, 2 tablespoonfuls of flour, 1 tablespoonful of sugar, 1 tablespoonful of salt and a little pepper. Bake in small cakes on griddle with plenty of butter. Serve hot.

Orange-Honey Carrots

1 bunch carrots, sliced
¼ cup melted butter
¼ cup honey
1 T grated orange rind

Cook carrots until tender. Drain. Blend butter, honey and orange rind. Pour over carrots and place on low heat until carrots are glazed.

Corn Pudding

Beat:
3 eggs
Add:
2 cups cream style corn
2 cups milk
⅛ tsp pepper
2 T butter
1 tsp salt
2 tsp sugar
Bake at 350° F. until golden brown.

Indian Corn

3 slices bacon, diced
1 can No. 2 (corn)
½ tsp salt
dash of pepper
3 eggs, slightly beaten
6 buttered toast rounds

Pan broil bacon until crisp, add corn and heat thoroughly. Add seasoning to eggs and pour over corn. Cook slowly, stirring occasionally until eggs are cooked. Serve on toast. 6 portions.

Potato Puffs

Two cups of mashed potatoes, 2 tablespoons of melted butter, mix these together to a cream, beat 2 eggs very light and add very scant pint of milk. Add this to the potato, season with salt and pepper, pour into a greased baking dish and bake for ½ hour until it browns nicely.

Potato Cake

6 cups mashed white potato
⅓ cup butter
3 eggs, separated
½ cup sugar
2 cups fresh cut corn pulp
½ tsp salt
Dash of pepper
A few gratings of nutmeg

Cream potato, add butter, nutmeg and egg yolk, beat thoroughly, add corn, stir well and lastly fold in stiffly beaten whites of eggs. Bake in a shallow pan. This will serve generously 8 people.

Baked Turnip Puff

2 cups hot mashed potatoes
2 cups hot mashed turnips
2 T butter
1 egg, well beaten
2 T sweet cream
½ tsp salt
⅛ tsp pepper

Mix potato and turnip. Add other ingredients. Turn into well greased baking dish and bake in moderately hot oven for 25 minutes. Serve hot in same dish. Serves six.

Diced Turnips

Pare, slice, cut in dice, 1 inch square, boil till nearly done in as little water as possible; to 1 quart of turnips add 1 tablespoon of sugar, salt to make it palatable; when they are boiled as dry as possible add 2 or 3 spoons of cream and 1 beaten egg.

Candied Sweet Potatoes

1 cup unsweetened pineapple juice
1 cup light brown sugar
½ cup white sugar
½ tsp salt
3 T butter

Bring the ingredients to a boil for 10 minutes. Peel cooked sweet potatoes. If large cut in halves. Add to the syrup and cook 20 to 25 minutes, turning occasionally. This is enough syrup for 10 to 12 sweet potatoes.

Sweet Potato Puffs

2 cups mashed sweet potato
1 T butter
1 egg
Salt and pepper
¼ cup milk or cream

To the mashed sweet potatoes, add the melted fat, seasonings and milk or cream. Beat the egg yolk and white separately. Add the yolk to the potato mixture and then fold in the white. Put into a casserole or individual molds. Cover with marshmallows. Set in a pan containing hot water and bake 375° until puffy and brown.

Oyster Cabbage

Cook the cabbage in water until well done and pour off the water; add ½ pint of milk thickened with rolled crackers. Season with butter, salt and pepper.

Escalloped Cauliflower

Boil till tender. Drain well and cut in small pieces. Put it in layers with fine chopped egg and this dressing: Half pint of milk thickened over boiling water with 2 tablespoonfuls of flour and seasoned with 2 teaspoons of salt, 1 of white pepper and 2 ounces of butter. Put grated bread over the top, dot it with small bits of butter and place it in the oven to heat thoroughly and brown. Serve in the same dish in which it was baked.

My neighbor, Wally Raich, learned a good lesson from green tomatoes.

"In Minnesota, up next to the Canadian border, we were poor as church mice during the Depression. But there were some who were even poorer. There was a widow down the road and my mother would have her come and eat with us from time to time because she knew the woman was destitute. One day the lady invited us back for dinner.

"All she had to put on the table were fried green tomatoes. I was five or six at the time and was about to open my mouth and complain about eating fried green tomatoes and nothing else. But I caught my mother's eye. I still remember that look. It said, plain as anything, 'If you say one word, young man, I will deal with you when we get home.'

"When I was older I realized how important it had been for us to eat with her. Only that way could she feel free to accept my mother's invitations."

Fried Green Tomatoes

Cut 6 large green tomatoes into slices about ⅛ of an inch thick. Beat the yolk of an egg with a tablespoonful of cold water. Sprinkle over the tomatoes some salt and pepper, dip them in the egg and then in fine bread crumbs. Fry in butter, brown thoroughly on both sides, and serve with a gravy made as follows: Rub together 1 tablespoonful of flour with 2 tablespoonfuls of butter, and when well creamed, brown in the pan; add ½ pint of boiling milk, stirring constantly until it begins to thicken; then add a saltspoonful of salt and pour over the tomatoes.

Stuffed Baked Tomatoes

6 tomatoes
3 T grated cheese
1 cup of bread crumbs (biscuit, light
    bread and very little corn bread)
2 level T of sugar
1 rounded T of butter
1 level tsp of salt
1 small onion, cut fine
¼ tsp celery seed
Black pepper to taste

Select smooth, medium sized tomatoes. Slice about one-half inch off stem end of each. Carefully remove meat of tomato with spoon, discarding hard parts around stem. Mix ingredients, stuff, bake 35 minutes at 350°.

Devilled Tomatoes

Large, firm tomatoes cut in ½" thick slices, sprinkle with flour on both sides and broil.

Pour over them the following sauce and serve at once.

Yolk of hard boiled egg
One whole egg
1 T vinegar
1 T melted butter
1 tsp sugar
1 tsp salt
½ tsp mustard
¼ tsp cayenne

Rub egg yolk with vinegar and butter and blend with seasonings and boil for one minute, then pour on a well beaten egg. Keep hot in a double boiler while broiling the tomatoes.

Beets with Orange Juice

1 T butter
4 T brown sugar
1½ T flour
¾ cup orange juice
Orange peel
⅛ tsp salt and paprika

Melt butter in double boiler. Add sugar mixed with flour and orange juice. Cook until thick. Add seasoning and 2½ cups beets. Heat.

Stuffed Onions

Remove skins, parboil 10 minutes in boiling salted water to cover. Turn upside down to cool, and remove part of center. Fill cavities with equal parts of finely chopped cooked chicken or veal, stale bread crumbs and finely chopped onion which was removed from center. Season with salt and pepper, moisten with cream or melted butter. Place in shallow baking dish, cover with buttered crumbs. Bake until onions are soft.

Stuffed Baked Onions

Boil large onions until tender, remove two-thirds of the onion in the center, fill with finely chopped apples, cinnamon and sugar. Bake in a moderate oven until the apples are tender.

Dressing for Boiled Beets

1 cup vinegar
1 T butter
¼ cup sweet cream
1 T sugar
Salt
1 tsp flour

Mix vinegar, butter and sugar. Bring to a boil, then add flour and cream which have been mixed together. Cook until slightly thickened. Pour over boiled, diced beets.

Swedish Spinach

Boil 2 lbs spinach in very little salted water until tender — no longer. Drain, rub through a coarse strainer and reheat with 1 cup rich cream.

Spinach Supreme

Partly line a baking dish with thin slices of bacon, cut in small squares. Fill with chopped cooked spinach mixed with equal parts of bread crumbs, 3 well beaten eggs, salt, dash of mace and ½ cup thin cream or rich milk. Lay bacon strips over top. Bake until bacon is crisp.

Carrots and String Beans

2 cups diced cooked carrots
1 cup cooked or canned string beans
½ tsp salt
3 T melted butter
1 cup milk
½ cup grated cheese
1 egg, beaten
1 cup bread crumbs
1 T melted butter

Combine ingredients, all but buttered crumbs. Place in baking dish, cover with crumbs and bake for 25 minutes in a moderate oven of 350°.

Green Beans with Dill

3 to 4 cups cut green beans
1 T minced parsley
2 T minced onions
1 T butter
½ tsp salt
1 T flour
1 tsp vinegar
2 T cream
1 tsp dill seed
dash of pepper

Cook beans in boiling salted water 15 minutes or until tender. Drain and reserve ¾ cup liquid. Melt butter; add flour and blend; add parsley, onion and bean liquid. Cook until thick. Add dill seed and seasonings. Simmer 5 minutes. Add beans, cream and vinegar. Serve at once.

Sauce for String Beans

Heat 2 cans beans in their own liquid. Drain and put into buttered casserole and top with the following sauce:
1 T butter
1 T flour
½ cup cream
1 can beef consommé

Melt butter. Blend in flour and cook until bubbly. Stir in cream and consommé. Heat through and pour over beans. Top with cracker crumbs. Bake 10 minutes at 350°. 4–6 servings.

Green Beans Southern Style

1 qt green beans
¾ cup cured ham (ground)
1 large cup tomatoes
1 small onion
1 T flour
Salt and pepper to season

Cook beans and ham together, ½ hour, with very little liquid. Put in casserole. Make a sauce by frying onion in bacon fat. Add the flour, then tomatoes, boil until thick. Pour over beans and bake ½ hour in moderate oven.

Scalloped Kidney Beans

2 cups cooked red kidney beans
⅓ cup raw rice
2 cups tomatoes
3 slices bacon (chopped)
¼ cup chopped raw onion
1 T sugar
1 tsp salt
Pepper

Parboil rice 5 minutes, drain. Put beans and rice in layers in buttered casserole. Brown bacon and onions, add tomatoes and seasoning. Pour over bean mixture and bake 30 minutes.

Glazed Baked Beans

1 lb navy beans
2 qts cold water
3 T cornstarch
1 T dark syrup
1 T molasses
1 T salt
1 cup ketchup
½ tsp pepper
¼ lb bacon, sliced

Soak beans in water overnight. Simmer in soaking water 1½ hours, not until mushy. Add more water if necessary to keep covered. Pour beans into shallow pan, after mixing with all other ingredients, except bacon. Arrange bacon slices on top of beans. Bake in moderate oven (350°) for 45 minutes, then stir beans and return to oven for 45 minutes longer.

Baked Beans

2 cups navy beans
¼ lb salt pork, bacon or pork sausage
1½ tsp salt
2 T molasses
¼ cup white or brown sugar
½ tsp mustard
1 small onion

Wash beans, cover with water and let stand overnight. Cook slowly until skins burst: Drain. Put all ingredients in baking dish. Cover with boiling water. Bake in slow oven 250° to 300° 6 to 7 hours. Add more water if necessary.

Boiling times have changed. The 1901 book of the Ladies of the Catholic Mite Society in LaConner said string beans should be boiled for an hour, spinach one to two hours, cabbage 45 minutes to two hours. Another old book gives boiling times much the same, adding that old beets should be boiled "forever."

Lima Beans au Gratin

4 slices bacon chopped
4 tsp flour
2½ cups lima beans
½ cup grated American cheese
¼ tsp salt
½ cup buttered bread crumbs

Fry bacon crisp. Blend with flour. Add beans and cheese. Season and cook until smooth and thickened. Place in baking dish. Top with crumbs and brown.

68

Relishes, Conserves

Chutney

8 ripe tomatoes
2 small red peppers
8 onions
8 apples

Grind together. Add:

2 cups sugar
1 tsp cloves
1 tsp cinnamon
1 cup vinegar
1 tsp salt

Boil 1½ hours and seal in jars.

Rhubarb Relish

1 qt chopped rhubarb
1 pt vinegar
1 qt onions, finely cut
1½ lbs brown sugar
1 tsp cinnamon
½ tsp allspice
½ tsp cloves
Dash of pepper

Boil ingredients until fairly thick. Remove
and seal in jars.

Tomato-Apple Relish

12 ripe tomatoes
12 large tart apples
9 good sized onions
2 cups white sugar
2 T salt
2 cups boiling vinegar
1 tsp each cinnamon and cloves
1 tsp each mustard, ginger and black
   pepper

Chop vegetables medium fine. Boil all
ingredients thoroughly. Seal.

Tomato Butter

7 lbs tomatoes, cut up
3 lbs sugar
1 pt vinegar
½ tsp cloves
1 tsp salt
1 tsp pepper
1 tsp cinnamon

Do not strain tomatoes as for catsup.

Green Tomato Relish

24 large green tomatoes
4 large green peppers
4 large red peppers
8 onions

Put all through meat grinder, and drain.

4 cups vinegar
1 cup water, or juice from above
4 cups sugar
4 tsp mustard seed
2 tsp celery seed
2 heaping T salt

Boil 10 minutes, or longer, until thick.

Pepper Relish

1 dozen red peppers
1 dozen green peppers
15 ground onions
1 handful salt

Remove the seeds from the peppers. Chop.
Combine all ingredients and cover with hot
water. Let stand four minutes and then
drain. Repeat and let stand ten minutes.
Drain. Place on stove with enough vinegar
to cover. Add 2 cups sugar and cook for 15
minutes. Seal in hot, sterilized jars.

Million Dollar Sauce

1 qt cucumbers, peeled and chopped
2 qts cabbage, chopped
1 qt onion

Add 1 cup salt. Let stand overnight and
drain in the morning. Make paste of:

1 pt vinegar
½ lb mustard
1 cup flour
1 tsp turmeric

Scald: 3 pints vinegar and add:

1 cup sugar
1 T celery seed
3 T white mustard seed

Pour in paste and stir until mixture
thickens. Add the vegetables and heat
well. Seal.

Chow Chow

3 heads of cabbage
12 green tomatoes
6 onions
Salt
½ gal vinegar
4 cups sugar
4 T mixed spices

Chop the cabbage, tomatoes and onions and put into a bowl. Sprinkle generously with salt and let stand overnight. Press out all the water and boil until tender in the vinegar, sugar and spices. (Put the spices in cloth bags.) Pack in hot, sterilized jars and seal.

Corn Salad

1 gal corn cut from cob
1 gal chopped cabbage
4 sweet peppers
4 large onions
4 cups sugar
½ cup salt (scant)
2 T celery seed
2 qt mild vinegar

Boil 20 minutes, seal while hot.

Mock Mince Meat

3 lbs green tomatoes
3 lbs apples, chopped
2 lbs raisins, chopped
8 cups brown sugar
2 tsp cloves
Orange peel
2 T salt
1 cup suet
1 cup vinegar
2 T cinnamon
1 tsp nutmeg

Chop tomatoes and drain. Measure juice and add equal amount of water to pulp. Scald mixture and drain liquid. Repeat twice the process of adding fresh water, scalding, and draining. To the mixture add apples, sugar, raisins, salt, and cook until clear. Add remaining ingredients and cook mixture until thick. Pack immediately in clean, hot jars and seal at once.

Ruby Relish

2 lbs medium size beets (about 9 beets)
1 small onion
½ red pepper
2 cups very finely chopped shredded cabbage
¼ cup prepared horseradish
1½ tsp salt
½ cup sugar
1½ cups vinegar

Pare beets. Grind beets, onion and red pepper, using fine blade of food chopper. Measure two cups. Add remaining ingredients; mix well. Heat to boiling. Simmer 10 minutes. Seal in hot sterilized jars. Makes two pints.

Beet-Apple Relish

10 medium beets, cooked
6 apples
1 large onion

Grind these and add 2½ cups sugar, 2 cups vinegar, 1 T salt, ½ tsp pepper, 1 tsp allspice. Boil till it thickens a little, seal in sterilized jars.

Mustard Pickles

1 head cauliflower
1 qt small green tomatoes
3 green peppers
2½ cups green limas
1 qt pickling onions
24 two-inch cucumbers
1 cup sugar
¾ cup flour
½ cup dry mustard
1 T turmeric
7 cups cider vinegar
7 cups water

Method: Break cauliflower in flowerettes, combine with tomatoes. Cut in wedges, peppers. Cut into strips, limas, onions and cucumbers. Cover with one cup coarse salt and four cups water; let stand overnight. Drain, cover with boiling water; let stand 10 minutes. Drain; combine remaining ingredients; cook until thick. Add vegetables; cook until just tender. Seal in hot sterilized jars. Makes eight pints.

Watermelon Rind Pickles

7 lbs watermelon rind
7 cups sugar
2 cups vinegar
½ tsp oil of cloves
½ tsp oil of cinnamon

Trim off dark green and pink parts of watermelon rind. Cut into inch cubes or cut with small biscuit cutter. Soak in lime water (1 tablespoon slaked lime to a quart of water) or in salt water (¼ cup salt to quart of water). Drain; rinse and cover with cold water. Cook until tender but not soft; drain. Combine sugar, vinegar, oil of cloves, oil of cinnamon and heat to boiling. Pour over rind, let stand overnight. In the morning drain off syrup. Heat and pour over rind. Repeat. The third morning, heat rind in syrup. Seal in hot, sterilized jars. The oils of cinnamon and cloves keep the rind clear and transparent. Makes 8 pints.

Melon Pickles with Lemon

Cut melon rind in long, thin slices or in 1 inch cubes. Soak and make a syrup of:

4 cups sugar
1 lemon, sliced very thin
1 pt vinegar

Add rind to pickling liquid and boil until clear. Seal while hot.

Sweet Pickled Carrots

2 cups vinegar
2 T mixed spices
1 cup sugar

Boil together for five minutes. Fill the jars with young, even sized carrots, boiled until tender, cover with the hot pickled syrup and seal at once.

(These cooks sealed their boiling hot preserves and relishes in jars sterilized in boiling water. Home economists today advise also processing in hot water bath to be certain of preventing spoilage. Check canning section of your standard cookbook.)

Dill Pickles

Soak medium sized cucumbers in cold water for eight hours. Put in jars with dill on top and bottom of jar. Heat three cups water, one-half cup vinegar, ¼ cup salt for each two quart jar. Add while hot and seal.

Sweet Pickles

Wash and dry 50 or 60 small cucumbers about four or five inches long. Cover with brine made of 1 pt salt, 1 gal water. Let stand one week. Drain and cover with boiling water to which has been added 1 T powdered alum. Let stand 24 hours. Drain. Split each cucumber. Cover with boiling water. Let stand 24 hours longer. Drain. Cover with following hot liquid: ½ oz celery seed, ½ oz stick cinnamon, 6 cups sugar, 5 pts vinegar. Let stand one week. Each morning for 3 mornings, drain off liquid and add 1 cup sugar. Heat liquid to boiling point and pour over pickles. Heat rest of liquid without adding sugar. Pack in jars and seal.

Sweet Jerken Pickles

Use 7 lbs cucumbers about 3 inches or smaller. Place in stone jar and cover with brine made of 1 pt salt, 1 gal cold water. Let stand 4 days. Then pour off water. Cover with clear cold water; let stand 3 days. Drain. Split pickles regardless how small. Put in kettle. Add 2 cups vinegar and water to cover, add handful green grape leaves or horseradish leaves, 1 tsp alum and simmer 2 hours. Pour off liquid. Put pickles back in stone jar. Heat 3 pts vinegar, 3 pts sugar, 1 oz whole allspice, 1 oz stick cinnamon. Pour this over pickles. Let stand overnight. Next morning heat liquid, pour over. Third morning pack in jars, pour liquid boiling hot over pickles and seal.

Pickled Beets

Select small young beets, cook until tender, dip into cold water. Peel off skins. Make the following syrup:

2 cups sugar
2 cups water
2 cups vinegar
1 tsp cloves
1 tsp allspice
1 thinly sliced lemon
1 T cinnamon

Pour over beets and simmer 15 minutes. Pack into sterilized jars and seal.

Baked Peach Pickles

48 small peaches
3 oranges
3 lemons
7 cups sugar
1 tsp oil of cloves

Peel peaches and put halves into baking pan. Slice oranges and lemons, put over peaches with sugar and bake till done. Put into jars. Into juice, put 1 tsp oil of cloves. Stir well. Pour over peaches and seal.

Cranberry Relish

2 medium-sized oranges
1 quart cranberries
2 cups sugar

Do not peel the oranges, but wash well and cut into thin slices. Removed all seeds. Add berries which have been well washed. Chop fine, or put through food chopper. Add sugar, place in glass dish. Cover and chill 24 hours.

Pickled Peaches

1 quart vinegar
3 pints white sugar
Cinnamon sticks
Whole cloves
Allspice

Let syrup cook some, then put in peaches. Cook until tender and place in glass jars and let syrup cook until quite rich. Pour over and seal.

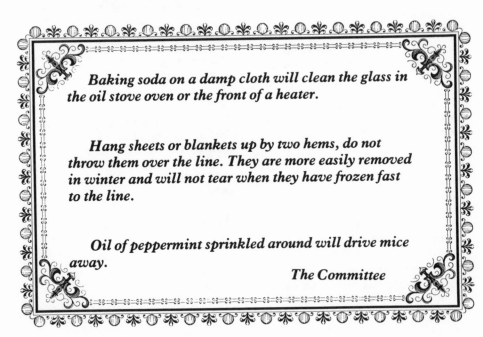

Baking soda on a damp cloth will clean the glass in the oil stove oven or the front of a heater.

Hang sheets or blankets up by two hems, do not throw them over the line. They are more easily removed in winter and will not tear when they have frozen fast to the line.

Oil of peppermint sprinkled around will drive mice away.

The Committee

Cherry Olives

1 pt water
1 pt vinegar if not too strong
2 T salt
1 T sugar

This cans 6 pints of cherries.

Strawberry Preserves

2 quarts strawberries
3 T vinegar
6 cups sugar

Cook berries and vinegar 3 minutes after it starts to boil. Add sugar and boil 10 minutes. Let stand 24 hours, stirring often. Put in jars and seal.

Rhubarb Date Jam

Cut up 7 cups rhubarb. Add 5 cups sugar and let stand overnight. In the morning add 1 pound dates, chopped; juice of one lemon, 2 oranges (juice and pulp), ½ teaspoon salt and boil till thick. The last 10 minutes add 1 cup nutmeats. Seal in pint jars while hot.

Mixed Fruit Jam

Combine ½ cup orange juice and ¼ cup lemon juice. Add 1 cup each of cut up peaches and cut up pears, 1 cup crushed pineapple and juice and ½ cup maraschino cherries, quartered. Add 5 cups sugar and let stand 1 hour. Bring to a boil and boil 1 minute. Add ½ cup pectin. Remove from heat and stir 5 minutes. Put in glasses.

Plum Conserve

1 lb plum pulp
1½ cups sugar
½ lemon, juice and grated rind
½ orange, juice and grated rind
1 cup seeded raisins
½ cup nut meats, if desired

Wash plums. Seed weigh, mix ingredients (except nuts) and cook mixture until thick and clear. Add nuts, pack into sterilized jars and seal.

Carrot Jam

Equal portions carrots and sugar
1 lemon to each cup carrots

Boil carrots until very tender. Mash fine. Add sugar and thinly sliced lemon. Cook on low heat about 3 hours. Stir occasionally.

Peach Conserve

14 peaches, peeled and diced
As much sugar as fruit
1 can shredded pineapple

Cook until clear and thick, stirring often to keep from burning. Put into sterilized jars and seal.

Rhubarb Marmelade

5 lbs rhubarb
8 cups sugar
2 oranges
2 cups walnuts

Wash rhubarb, cut in pieces and pour boiling water over it. Allow to stand 3 minutes and drain. Add sugar, grated rind and juice of oranges. Cook slowly till thick. Add chopped nuts and pour into sterilized jars.

Yellow Tomato Preserve

12 large yellow tomatoes
8 cups sugar
2 oranges
1 lemon

Use both inside and outside rind of lemon and oranges. Cook until thick.

Cookies

Hurrying through the mall, I bought a small package of paper-thin, cracker-crisp white cookies at a bake sale table. "Those are called 'Million Dollar Cookies,' " said the woman behind the table.

I brought them to Althea at the nursing home. Althea, not one to waste words, took a bite and said, "Better get the recipe for these."

But I wasn't able to track down the sale group and the "Million Dollar" member. But weeks later, in *Knapp's Tasty Recipes* (North Crow River Church, Minnesota), I found "Million Dollar Cookies" by Edna Melin Peterson. I baked some and brought them to the nursing home. Althea munched one thoughtfully and finally announced, "They're close."

Omit the nuts (or grind them very fine) and press the cookies very, very thin, and I think she's right. They're close.

Million Dollar Cookies

1 cup shortening (I used half butter, half
   margarine)
½ cup white sugar
½ cup brown sugar
1 tsp soda
1 tsp salt
1 egg
2 cups flour
1 tsp vanilla
½ cup chopped nuts

Cream shortening, add sugar and beaten egg. Add sifted dry ingredients and lastly the finely chopped nuts. Form into balls, roll in granulated sugar and flatten with a glass dipped in sugar. Bake at 350 degrees 10 to 12 minutes.

Sugar Cookies

2 cups sugar
1 cup butter
1 cup sour cream
3 eggs
1 tsp vanilla
1 tsp soda

Flour to make dough to handle. Mix and roll thin. Sift sugar over and gently roll in. (We would say "roll out." Bake at 350° about 12 minutes.)

Sugar Cookies

1 cup shortening
1½ cups sugar
2 eggs
3 cups sifted flour
½ tsp salt
½ tsp baking powder
¼ cup milk
1½ tsp vanilla

Roll very thin. Sprinkle with sugar or brush with milk and cut. Bake 5 to 9 minutes in 425° oven.

White Rolled Out Cookies

1 cup sugar
1 cup lard
½ tsp salt
2 eggs
4 T milk
3 cups flour
½ tsp nutmeg
1 tsp soda
2 tsp baking powder

Cream the first two ingredients. Mix the rest in the order given. Chill. Roll out, cut, and bake about 10–15 minutes at 400°. (These work well for Christmas cookies such as stars, bells, etc. and can be decorated with frostings or colored sugar.)

Aunt Mary's Cookies

2 cups white sugar
2 cups butter
4 eggs (well beaten)
5 cups flour
2 tsp soda
4 tsp cream of tartar
1 tsp salt
Flavor to taste (1 tsp nutmeg or 1 tsp
    vanilla or lemon)

Roll not too thin and sprinkle with white
sugar. Bake 10 minutes in quick oven. For
a change, press a raisin or nut meat in
center of each.

Soft Ginger Cookies

1 cup sugar
1 cup lard
½ cup molasses
1 cup sour milk
1 tsp soda in milk
1 tsp ginger
½ tsp cloves and cinnamon
1 tsp baking powder in
Flour enough to roll

Rolled Oatmeal Cookies

1¼ cups butter or shortening
2 cups brown sugar
2 eggs beaten
¾ cup sour milk
1 tsp soda
2 tsp vanilla
½ tsp salt (less if butter is used)
2 cups raisins (ground)
4 cups coarse oatmeal (ground)
3 cups flour

Mix in order given and roll out thin. Cut
with cookie cutter and bake at 350° for
8–10 minutes or until done.

Hermits

One cup of butter, 3 cups of brown sugar,
4 tablespoonfuls of milk, 4 eggs, 2
teaspoons of soda, 2 cups of raisins, 2 cups
of currants, 1 cup of nuts, 1 teaspoon of
grated nutmeg, 1 teaspoon of cinnamon, a
little grated orange peel, a cup of flour,
drop in buttered pan and bake.

*Recipes for "rocks" and "hermits" are used
interchangeably, though "rocks" are more
likely to call for oatmeal. Where the name
"hermit" came from no one seems to know.
Some recipes included dates and were called
"Honolulu Hermits." A 1906 cookbook ended
its recipe, "You may stick a currant in the top
for The Hermit." Did the cookie represent a
hermit guru living at the top of a mountain?*

Sugar Cookies

Mix together:
½ cup shortening
½ cup sugar
½ tsp grated lemon rind (or orange rind)
¼ tsp salt

Add and mix well:
1 egg, unbeaten
2 T milk

Sift in:
2 cups flour
½ tsp soda
½ tsp baking powder

Drop by teaspoonful on greased cookie
sheet. Grease bottom of a glass and dip in
sugar. Press each cookie flat with bottom
of sugar coated glass. Sprinkle nutmeg on
cookies. Bake 8 to 10 minutes at 400°.
Makes 3 dozen.

Date Oatmeal Cookies

1½ cups brown sugar
1 cup shortening
2 eggs
½ cup shredded coconut
½ cup walnut meats
1 cup uncooked oats
1 tsp vanilla
1 tsp soda
1 lb dates
2 cups flour using last ½ to flour dates

Drop from spoon. Bake.

Oatmeal Cookies

½ cup butter
½ cup lard
1 cup sugar
2 eggs, well beaten
½ tsp salt
½ tsp cinnamon
½ tsp cloves
1 tsp soda
2 cups flour
⅓ cup milk
½ cup walnuts
1½ cups raisins
1½ cups oatmeal

Cream butter, lard and sugar. Add eggs. Sift together salt, cinnamon, cloves, soda, flour. Add dry ingredients alternately with milk to batter. Add walnuts, raisins and oatmeal. Mix well and drop from spoon onto cookie sheet and bake in moderately hot oven.

Chocolate Chip Oatmeal Cookies

1 cup shortening
¾ cup white sugar
¾ cup brown sugar
2 cups quick oatmeal
1 pkg chocolate chips
2 cups flour (sift before measuring)
2 beaten eggs
1 tsp vanilla
1 tsp salt
1 tsp soda
1 cup chopped nuts

Mix thoroughly. Drop by teaspoonful on cookie sheet. Bake at 350° for 13 to 15 minutes.

Ranger Cookies

1 cup shortening
1 cup white sugar
1 cup brown sugar
2 eggs
1 tsp vanilla
1 tsp soda
½ tsp baking powder
½ tsp salt
2 cups flour
2 cups oatmeal
2 cups rice krispies
1 cup shredded coconut
1 pkg chocolate chips

Cream together the shortening and sugar. Add eggs and vanilla. Sift together the soda, baking powder, salt and flour and add to mixture. Add oatmeal, rice krispies, coconut and chips. Dough will be crumbly. Place on cookie sheet and bake in moderate oven.

Raisin Cookies

1 cup raisins
1 cup cold water
1½ cups sugar
½ cup shortening
1 egg
1 tsp cinnamon
½ tsp nutmeg
Pinch of salt
3 cups flour
1 tsp soda
1 cup coconut or nuts if desired

Cook raisins in water for few minutes. Cool. Drain water from raisins — add enough to make 1 cup liquid. Add to remaining ingredients. Drop by spoonfuls on cookie sheet and bake.

Grandma's Sour Cream Rocks

2 cups brown sugar
1 cup butter
3 eggs, beaten
½ cup sour cream
2 tsp soda (scant)
1 tsp cinnamon
4 cups flour
Raisins and nuts

Cream sugar and butter; stir in eggs. Sift together dry ingredients and add alternately with sour cream. Stir in raisins and nuts. Drop by teaspoon on cookie sheet. Bake in 375° oven until golden brown.

During the Vietnam War we baked Mrs. Levy's Cookies. I think Mrs. Levy lived in Chicago. At any rate, she baked prodigious amounts of cookies for service people in Vietnam and had developed a recipe that tasted good, traveled well and stayed reasonably fresh even if it took a month or more for the box to reach its destination. The recipe was published all over the country and thousands of veterans must remember Mrs. Levy's Cookies:

Mrs. Levy's Cookies

¾ cup shortening
1 cup brown sugar
1 egg
1½ cups flour
½ teaspoon soda
1 teaspoon cinnamon
¼ teaspoon nutmeg
½ cup walnuts
½ cup chocolate chips (mint if available)

½ cup coconut
½ cup raisins
1 cup mashed ripe banana (2 or 3 bananas)
1¾ cups rolled oats (quick cooking)

Mix first three ingredients till creamy. Sift and add dry ingredients, then rest of ingredients. Drop from spoon on greased tins. Bake at 375 for about 12 minutes.

But there's an older cookie recipe. Julia Prescott Ekstrand found a cookbook in her late mother's collection that had belonged to her Grandmother Houghton, who died in 1937 at the age of 85. "The Princess Cookbook" was put out by the Ladies Aid of the Christian Church in Whitten, Iowa, sometime before the turn of the century and has recipes for gooseberry catsup, preserved eggs, jellied pigs feet, vinegar pie and Prince of Wales Cake, to name a few.

Tucked in its brittle, yellowed pages is an equally yellowed sheet of old, wide-lined tablet paper. On it, in a fine, precise hand, is written,

"Soldier Boy Cookies, A Hoard's Dairyman Prize-Winning Recipe." (Hoard's Dairyman was an old farm magazine.) And at the end of the recipe the unknown correspondent has written,

"This recipe was used nearly 70 years ago by a mother who sent these cookies to her son who fought in the Civil War. This recipe made my roaster full of cookies. I used orange rind to flavor them." The recipe follows:

Soldier Boy Cookies

3 cups sugar
1 cup butter
2 cups thick sour cream
1 teaspoonful soda
3 eggs
1 teaspoonful ginger or 1 teaspoon vanilla

and grated rind of one orange.
Flour to make a smooth dough (about 3½ cups)
Roll thin, sprinkle with sugar, cut and bake.

The note is probably from around 1905. Some 40 years later, in the 1947 book of the Miriam Society in Buffalo, Minnesota, is a similar recipe also titled "Soldier Boy Cookies." It calls for one less cup of sugar (war years influence?), two teaspoons of soda and ginger or lemon flavoring.

Stone Jar Nut Cookies

1 cup shortening
1 tsp salt
1 tsp vanilla
1 tsp nutmeg
2 cups brown sugar, firmly packed
2 eggs, well beaten
3 cups sifted flour
1 tsp soda
¼ cup milk
1 cup nuts, chopped

Combine shortening, salt, vanilla and
nutmeg. Add brown sugar gradually and
cream well. Add beaten eggs and mix
thoroughly. Sift flour with soda. Add half
of flour to creamed mixture, then add
milk, then remaining flour and nuts,
mixing well. Drop from teaspoon on
greased baking sheets. Let stand a few
minutes, then flatten cookies by stamping
with a glass covered with a damp cloth.
Bake in a moderately hot oven (375°) for 8
to 10 minutes. Makes 6 dozen cookies.

Pumpkin Cookies

1 cup shortening
½ cup brown sugar
½ cup honey
1 egg
1 cup pumpkin
½ tsp baking powder
2 cups sifted flour
½ tsp soda
½ tsp salt
½ tsp each cloves, ginger, cinnamon and
    nutmeg
1 cup chopped nuts
1 cup raisins

Cream together shortening, brown sugar
and honey. When mixture is light and
fluffy, add egg and beat well. Add
pumpkin alternately with flour sifted
together with baking powder, soda, salt
and spices, blending well after each
addition. Stir in the nuts and raisins. Drop
by teaspoonfuls onto a well greased cookie
sheet. Bake in moderate oven (375°) for 15
to 18 minutes, or until cookies are done
and lightly browned. Makes 6 dozen.

Carrot Cookies

¾ cup shortening
1 egg
1 cup mashed carrots
2 cups sifted flour
2 tsp baking powder
¾ cup sugar
1 tsp vanilla
1 tsp lemon extract
½ tsp salt

Mix in order given. Bake at 375°. Frost
with powdered sugar, 1 teaspoon butter,
grated orange or lemon rind, and thin with
lemon juice.

Soft Rocks

1 cup dates, chopped
1 cup raisins
Water
1½ cups brown sugar
1 cup shortening (½ butter)
2 eggs
1 tsp soda in ¼ cup hot water
1 tsp vanilla
1 tsp salt
2 cups flour (soft dough)

Combine dates and raisins in water and
boil until they get thick. Cool. Cream
sugar and shortening; add eggs, salt and
soda dissolved in hot water. Add flour and
mix. Add vanilla, dates and raisins. Drop
by teaspoonfuls on buttered cookie sheet
and bake in 350° oven about 10 to 15
minutes. Can add walnuts on top for a
fancy cookie.

Snickerdoodles

Mix together thoroughly:

1 cup soft shortening
2 eggs
1½ cups sugar

Sift together and stir in:

2¾ cups flour
2 tsp cream of tartar
1 tsp soda
½ tsp salt

Chill dough. Roll into balls the size of small walnuts. Roll in mixture of 2 tablespoons sugar and 2 teaspoons cinnamon. Place on ungreased baking sheet 2 inches apart. Bake until light brown but still soft. Bake 8–10 minutes at 400°.

Sour Cream Cookies

2 cups sugar
1 cup shortening
3 eggs
1 cup sour cream
1 tsp vanilla
½ tsp soda
4 tsp baking powder
4½ cups sifted all-purpose flour
¼ tsp salt
½ cup coarsely chopped hickory nuts

Cream together sugar and shortening, add eggs one at a time, beating until well blended. Stir in sour cream and vanilla. Sift together soda, baking powder, flour and salt, stir into egg and sugar mixture. Drop batter by tablespoonfuls on greased cookie sheet. Sprinkle with nuts. Bake in moderate oven (350°) 20 minutes. These cookies should be large and fairly thick.

Finnish Cookies

1 cup butter
¼ cup sugar
2¼ cups flour

Mix well. Roll, or mold when stiff. Cut and dip in white of egg and chopped almond and crushed sugar. Bake at 350° 12 minutes.

Applesauce Cookies

1 cup brown sugar
½ cup vegetable fat or butter
1 cup applesauce
1 scant tsp soda
2 cups pre-sifted flour
1 tsp baking powder
½ tsp salt
½ tsp allspice
1 tsp cinnamon
1 cup raisins
1 cup walnuts

Cream shortening and sugar. Add applesauce mixed with a teaspoon of soda, then flour mixed with one teaspoon baking powder. Combine with rest of ingredients. Bake as small drop cookies in 350° oven.

Chocolate Drop Cookies

2 cups brown sugar
1 cup shortening, part butter
2 eggs
3 squares melted chocolate
1 cup sour milk
3 cups flour
1 tsp soda
¾ tsp salt
1 tsp vanilla
½ cup nuts
½ cup dates

Cream shortening and sugar and add eggs one at a time. Add melted chocolate. Sift together dry ingredients and add alternately with milk. Add vanilla, nuts, and dates. Drop on cookie sheet and bake at 375° for 10 to 15 minutes. Makes 4 dozen. Frost with any chocolate frosting.

All-Bran Butterscotch Ice Box Cookies

½ lb butter
2 cups brown sugar
2 eggs, beaten
1 cup all-bran
3 cups flour
2 tsp baking powder

Shape into rolls. Put in refrigerator overnight. Slice and bake.

Overnight Cookies

1 cup brown sugar
1 cup white sugar
1 cup butter
1 cup lard
3 eggs, beaten separately
1 tsp soda
1 tsp cinnamon
6½ cups flour
1 cup nuts

Knead flour in by hand. Roll into loaves and let stand in a cool place overnight. Slice and bake.

Crisp Oatmeal Cookies

3 cups oatmeal
1 cup brown sugar
¼ cup boiling water
1 tsp vanilla
½ tsp salt
1 cup flour
1 cup butter*
1 tsp soda

Mix oats, sugar, flour together. Add melted butter and soda dissolved in water. Form into roll. Chill and slice. Bake.

* Use part butter substitute and butter flavor.

Oatmeal Crispies

1 cup shortening
1 cup brown sugar
1 cup granulated sugar
2 eggs well beaten
1 tsp vanilla
½ tsp cinnamon
1⅔ cups sifted flour
1 tsp salt
1 tsp soda
3 cups quick oatmeal
½ cup chopped walnuts

Cream shortening and sugar thoroughly, add beaten eggs and oatmeal. Sift remaining dry ingredients, add along with chopped nuts and vanilla. Mix well and shape into rolls, place in refrigerator. Slice and bake on cookie sheet at 400° for 10 to 12 minutes.

Lemon and Coconut Ice Box Cookies

1 cup shortening
1 cup white sugar
1 cup brown sugar
2 well beaten eggs
2 T lemon juice
Grated rind of 1 lemon
1 tsp soda
1 tsp cream of tartar
¾ cup shredded coconut
4 cups flour

Cream shortening and sugar well. Add remaining ingredients. Mix well and make into two rolls. Put in refrigerator for several hours, then slice and bake in moderate oven.

Holland Dandies

½ lb butter
½ lb lard
1 cup sugar
1 qt sorghum
1 tsp salt
4 tsp cinnamon
1 tsp cloves
1 tsp nutmeg
¼ lb citron, finely chopped
2 cups nuts, chopped
5 tsp soda in ⅓ cup water
Flour

Mix ingredients in order given, using enough flour to make a soft dough. Pack in stone jar or crock and cover. This cookie dough, if kept in a cool place, will keep all winter. When cookies are needed, cut off the amount of dough required, form into a loaf and slice. Bake on a greased tin in a moderate oven.

Regular Service Between

New York

and

Norway

DIRECT calling at Bergen, Stavanger, Kristianssand and Oslo.

Through Bookings to Sweden, Denmark, Finland and the Continent

MODERN TWIN SCREW STEAMERS

"Stavangerfjord" — 13,156 Gross Tonnage, 18,000 Tons Displ.

"Bergensfjord" — 11,012 Gross Tonnage, 16,000 Tons Displ.

Free railway journey between Bergen and Oslo. Annual cruises to North Cape and Norwegian Fjords.

For further particulars, apply to local agent or to

NORWEGIAN AMERICA LINE

319 Second Ave. S.   **Minneapolis, Minn.**

—1926 book, Minneapolis. (See page 146)

Peanut Butter Cookies

Cream:

1 cup shortening
1 cup peanut butter
1 cup brown sugar
1 cup white sugar

Add:

2 well beaten eggs
2 tsp vanilla

Stir vigorously. Sift flour and measure 2½ cups flour. Sift again and add 2 teaspoons soda and ½ teaspoon salt. Add flour to first mixture and stir until all ingredients are thoroughly blended. Chill dough, then form into balls on lightly greased pan which has also been slightly dusted with flour. Flatten each ball with a fork which has been dipped in flour, forming a criss-cross pattern. Bake 10 to 12 minutes. Will make 4 dozen cookies.

Butterscotch Almond Cookies

1 cup brown sugar
1 cup white sugar
1½ cups butter and lard
2 eggs
1 tsp soda in 2 T vinegar
4 cups flour
⅛ tsp salt
1 tsp vanilla
1 tsp almond
½ cup chopped nuts

Roll in balls size of walnut. Press with the fork and criss-cross. Bake in hot oven.

Snowballs

1 cup butter and Crisco
¼ cup honey
⅓ tsp salt
2 cups flour
2 tsp vanilla
1 cup any nuts, chopped fine

Cream butter and honey, add flour, salt, and vanilla. Mix well. Add nuts and form into small balls. Bake 30 minutes in very slow oven. (Should not be brown.) While still hot roll in powdered sugar. Roll again in powdered sugar when cool.

Delight Bites

½ cup peanut butter
1 tsp butter
1 cup powdered sugar
6 glazed cherries cut very fine

Work with hands for a long time. Roll into small balls. Melt 4 squares of chocolate and 2 teaspoons parawax. Dip balls in chocolate mixture. Roll in fine nuts or coconut. Makes 24 to 30.

Mexican Wedding Cake

1½ cups butter or shortening
⅔ cup white sugar
4 cups flour
2 tsp vanilla
10 T powdered sugar
2 cups chopped nuts
2 tsp ice water

Roll in balls, bake 20 to 30 minutes at 300°. White when done.

Pecan Dreams

1 cup shortening
4 heaping T powdered sugar
1 T cold water
1 tsp vanilla
2 cups flour sifted
1 cup pecans, cut coarse

Cream shortening, add sugar, water, flour, vanilla and nuts. Roll in balls. Bake 25 minutes in slow oven. When done, cool and roll in powdered sugar.

Peanut Butter Balls

1 cup peanut butter
1 cup powdered sugar
1 T butter
1 cup chopped nuts
1 cup chopped dates

Roll in small balls and dip in the following ingredients, melted in double boiler.

1 pkg chocolate chips
2 squares bittersweet chocolate
1 square inch (paraffin) wax

Roll balls in chocolate and place on wax paper to cool.

Tomahawk Cookies

½ cup butter
½ cup Crisco
2 beaten eggs
1 cup brown sugar
1 cup white sugar
2½ cups flour
1 cup Rice Krispies
1 cup coconut
½ cup oatmeal
1 tsp soda
1 cup plain peanuts
1 tsp salt

Roll in balls and flatten with a fork. Bake.

Ginger Snaps

¾ cup shortening
1 cup sugar
1 egg beaten
4 T molasses
2 tsp soda
2½ cups flour
1 tsp ginger
1 tsp cloves
1 tsp cinnamon
¼ tsp salt

Mix all dry ingredients. Cream shortening and sugar. Add beaten eggs and molasses. Add to dry ingredients. Roll batter into ball size of small walnut. Dip one side of ball into sugar. Bake in moderate oven for 15 minutes.

Grandma's Ginger Snaps

1 cup sugar
⅔ cup shortening
2 eggs, beaten
1 cup molasses
2 tsp soda
1 tsp cinnamon
1 T ginger
1 pinch cloves
3¼ cups flour

Cream sugar and shortening, add well beaten eggs and molasses. Sift together the dry ingredients and stir into the creamed mixture. Mix well. Roll into balls size of marbles and bake in 375° oven one inch apart, 10 to 15 minutes.

Melting Moments Cookies

1 cup soft butter
⅓ cup powdered sugar
¾ cup cornstarch
1 cup flour

Cream butter, gradually add powdered sugar, then cornstarch and flour. Mix well. Chill 1 hour. Form into 36 small balls. Bake on ungreased cookie sheet at 350° about 15 minutes. When cool, frost with the following frosting.

2 T melted butter
1 cup powdered sugar
1 tsp flavoring, vanilla, lemon or orange
Cream enough to spread

Or:

1 cup powdered sugar
1 tsp soft butter
Juice of ½ lemon

Blend and swirl on cookies. Makes 4 dozen.

Cinnamon Thumbs

5 T white sugar
1 cup butter
2 cups flour
1 tsp vanilla
½ tsp salt
1 tsp almond (optional)

Roll in oblong shape like a ladyfinger about 1½ inches long. Press slightly. Bake in 350° oven from 10 to 12 minutes. While hot, roll in cinnamon and sugar mixture.

½ cup sugar
¼ tsp cinnamon

Porcupine Cookies

½ cup sugar
1 T butter
1 egg, beaten
1 tsp vanilla
1 cup chopped nuts
1 cup chopped dates

Cream butter and sugar, add egg and vanilla. Then dates and nuts. Roll in chopped coconut and bake in slow oven (275°) until delicately brown.

Graham Crackers

¾ cup brown sugar
½ cup shortening
1 quart graham flour
2 tsp baking powder
Salt to taste

Combine all ingredients and wet with milk. Roll out thin and cut in strips with knife, using white flour for rolling out. Bake in a quick oven. Good with a peanut butter or powdered sugar frosting or with a date filling.

Dishpan Cookies

2 cups brown sugar
2 cups white sugar
2 cups oil
4 eggs
2 tsp vanilla
4 cups flour
1½ cups oats
2 tsp baking soda
4 cups corn flakes
1 tsp salt

In large bowl cream sugar, oil, eggs and vanilla. Add flour, oats, baking soda, corn flakes and salt. If batter is stiff add small amount of milk. Drop off by teaspoon. Bake on ungreased cookie sheets at 350° for 8 to 10 minutes.

Frying Pan Cookies

¾ cup sugar
1 cup chopped dates
2 egg yolks, beaten creamy

Cook this mixture in a frying pan until the mixture pulls away from the pan (about 5 minutes). Cool 3 minutes, then add:

1 tsp vanilla
1 cup chopped nuts
1 cup corn flakes
1 cup Rice Krispies

Roll in small balls and roll in fine coconut. No baking required.

Marguerites

Make a meringue by beating one egg white until stiff. Add 3 teaspoons sugar. Spread rather thick on soda or graham crackers. Bake in a moderate oven until delicately browned. Nuts may be placed on top just before putting in oven. Serve with tea.

No Bake Apricot Balls

⅔ cup sweetened condensed milk
2 cups coconut
1 lb dried apricots ground in meat grinder

Mix well. Roll into little balls and roll in powdered sugar. Keep in refrigerator.

Unbaked Chocolate Cookies

2 eggs (well beaten)
2 cups powdered sugar
1 cup chopped nuts
40 marshmallows (cut up)
3 squares chocolate
1 tsp vanilla
Pinch of salt
Flaked coconut

Add sugar to well beaten eggs, then add nuts, marshmallows and chocolate (melted and cooled), then vanilla and salt. Make small balls and roll in coconut. Leave to harden.

Chinese Chews

3 eggs, beaten
1 cup sugar, add gradually
¾ cup flour
1 tsp baking flour
2 cups dates, chopped
1 cup chopped walnuts
Pinch of salt
Vanilla

Bake in large pan in slow oven about 20 minutes. Cut in squares before real cold, squeeze each square into a ball. Roll in granulated sugar.

Pin Wheel Cookies

½ cup sugar
½ cup butter
1 egg yolk
3 T milk
1½ cups flour
1½ tsp baking powder
½ tsp vanilla
⅛ tsp salt

Divide dough in half. Add 2 tablespoons cocoa to half. Roll each into a rectangle, quite thin. Cut each in half. Lay one on the other with light dough on the outside and straight edges together. Roll. Chill, slice and bake.

Date Pinwheels

1 cup brown sugar
3 eggs
3½ cups flour
1 tsp soda
1 cup shortening
1 cup white sugar
1 tsp cinnamon
¼ tsp salt

Cream sugars and shortening. Add eggs; beat well. Add dry ingredients. Chill dough well. Divide into thirds. Roll out and spread with date mixture. Roll as for jelly roll and chill well. Slice and bake on greased cookie sheet in 350° oven 12–15 minutes.

Date Filling: About 1 cup or more finely chopped dates, ½ cup white sugar, ½ cup water, 1 cup chopped nuts. Cook dates, sugar and water until thick. Cool and add chopped nuts.

Filled Date Crisps

1 cup brown sugar
1 cup butter
1 cup cream (sour)
¼ tsp salt
2 cups flour
1 tsp soda
2 cups rolled oats

Sift flour with soda and salt, add oatmeal. Cream butter and sugar, add dry ingredients alternately with sour cream

(chill). Roll thin and cut. Bake in moderate oven (350°) until brown. When baked put two cookies together with date filling.

½ lb dates
½ cup sugar
water to cover, cook until thick

Filled Cookies

1 cup sugar
¾ cup butter or substitute
¼ cup milk
2 eggs well beaten
3 tsp baking powder
Pinch of salt
1 tsp flavoring
Flour enough to roll
Filling:
1 cup ground dates or raisins
¾ cup sugar
2 T flour
1 cup boiling water

Cook until quite thick. Roll the cookies rather thin; cut out and put a teaspoon of filling on each cookie; then place another one on top, pressing the edge together. Mincemeat may also be used as a filling.

Fig Newtons

½ cup shortening
½ cup honey or syrup
½ cup sugar
1 egg
Juice and rind of ½ lemon
3¼ cups flour
1 tsp baking powder
½ tsp soda
½ tsp salt

Cream fat, sugar and honey. Add beaten egg and lemon juice and rind. Add flour with baking powder, soda and salt. Roll dough quite thin and cut into strips about 6 inches long by 3 inches wide. Spread filling in center of each strip and fold over and cut into desired lengths. Filling: 2 cups figs or dates, ½ cup honey, ½ cup water and juice of ½ lemon. Mix and cook, stirring constantly. Cool before spreading on dough.

At the time my husband and I were married, my friend Mary Mainquist (later Olson) worked in the Clerk of Court's office in Buffalo, Minnesota. She offered to bring the license with her to the wedding, saving us a trip back to pick it up after the waiting period. But the church was four miles out in the country, it was a very dark night and Mary took a wrong turn. Nervously the organist played on and on while we paced the floor in the church basement until a most welcome Mary came flying through the door.

Now, some 50 years later, Vivian Wilson of Geneva, Illinois, has sent me a cookbook published in 1947 by the Miriams Young Women's Missionary Society of Zion Lutheran Church in Buffalo, Minnesota. On the most worn, stained and yellowed page she has written, "This is the page I use every Christmas. Allen asks me why only at Christmas?"

She has circled one recipe, "Frosted Chocolate Drops," and penciled in beside it, "Ann would say they're dreamy."

The recipe is signed, "Mary Mainquist." Here it is:

1¼ cups flour
½ teaspoon baking soda
½ teaspoon salt
½ cup butter or shortening
2 squares unsweetened chocolate
1 teaspoon vanilla
½ cup nutmeats, chopped
1 egg

Sift flour, soda and salt together three times. Cream butter until lemon colored, add sugar gradually, beating after each addition. Slowly add well beaten egg and chocolate which has been melted and cooled. Stir vanilla into milk. Alternately add dry ingredients and liquid, beating after each addition. Stir in nutmeats. Drop by spoonfuls on ungreased baking sheet. Bake in hot oven (Vivian notes 350°) 8 to 10 minutes. When cool frost with soft chocolate frosting.

The women of the Congregational Church in Ann Arbor, Michigan, published the second edition of their cookbook in 1904, "revised and enlarged."

They were of sterner stuff than we. Not only does the lebkuchen recipe require stirring eggs and flour "in one direction for one-half hour," but the recipe for anis bröd, or Anise Cakes, tells us to stir eight eggs and a pound of sugar "in one direction for one-half hour." To this add a scant pound of flour, a teaspoon of baking powder and a tablespoonful of anise seed, plus enough more flour to make it easy to roll out thin as for ginger snaps.

And in the same section Mrs. Schlotterbeck gives us directions for Christmas cookies:

"One gallon molasses, ½ pint sour milk or cream, 2 cups lard, 2 pounds brown sugar, 5 tablespoons soda, 3 tablespoons cinnamon, a grated nutmeg; add citron, nuts, lemon and orange peel. Stir in flour until no more can be added, and let it stand overnight."

The good lady doesn't tell us what to do with it in the morning. Likely it's to be rolled out and cut with cookie cutters.

Lebkuchen

Four eggs, 1 pound of flour, beat in one direction ½ hour; ½ pound of crushed almonds, ¼ pound of sliced citron, 1 lemon, 1 orange, ½ an ounce of cinnamon, ¼ teaspoonful of cloves, 1 teaspoonful of allspice, ½ scant teaspoon of baking powder, ½ cup of molasses. Cream the eggs and sugar. Mix the almonds and flour and add to the previous mixture; grate into it the peel of 1 lemon and the orange, stir all together, adding the juice of each; stir in the molasses (or honey is better), then add lastly the baking powder. Stir hard and well; roll out, and cut into small rounds and squares. Bake in a moderate oven. When cold, spread lightly with frosting. Will keep any length of time. These will serve five people about 1 dozen times.

Apple Nut Bars

1 cup flour, sifted
1 tsp baking powder
¼ tsp salt
½ tsp cinnamon
¼ cup butter or margarine
¾ cup sugar
1 egg
1 tsp vanilla
1 apple, chopped
½ cup chopped nuts

Melt butter in saucepan, add sugar. Add egg and beat thoroughly. Add vanilla. Sift together flour, baking powder, salt and cinnamon and fold into butter mixture. Add nuts and chopped apple. Put in 8 × 8 greased pan. Bake at 350° for 30 minutes.

Applesauce Brownies

1 cup sugar
2 eggs
½ cup unsweetened applesauce
¼ tsp soda
½ tsp baking powder
1 tsp vanilla
7 T shortening
2 squares bitter chocolate
1 cup flour

¼ tsp salt
½ cup chopped nuts

Cream shortening and add the sugar. Then add beaten eggs and melted chocolate and beat well. Dissolve the soda in the applesauce and add to the first mixture and mix well. Add flour, baking powder, and salt which have been sifted together. Then add the nuts and the vanilla. Bake at 350°. Remove from oven and cut in squares.

Oatmeal Bars

4 cups oatmeal
1 tsp vanilla
¼ cup light corn syrup or honey
1 cup brown sugar
⅔ cup melted butter

Mix all together and pat in (9″ × 12″) pan. Bake about 15 minutes. Frost while warm with 1 cup chocolate chips and ⅔ cup crunchy peanut butter melted together.

Pumpkin Bars

1¾ cups flour
1 tsp baking soda
1½ tsp cinnamon
½ tsp nutmeg
¼ tsp cloves
¼ tsp salt
1 cup pumpkin puree
1 cup brown sugar, packed
1 egg
⅓ cup oil
1 cup chopped nuts
1 cup golden raisins

Blend first 6 ingredients, mix with rest all at once. Stir only till well blended. Spread in 10 by 15 inch pan, greased; bake at 350° about 20 minutes. Frost with powdered sugar frosting.

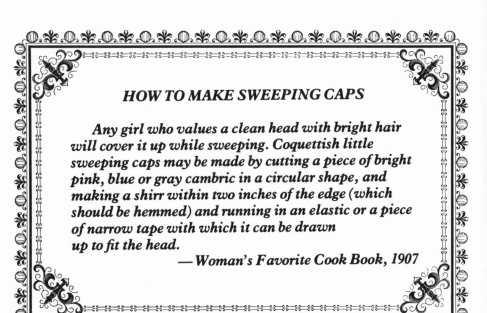

HOW TO MAKE SWEEPING CAPS

Any girl who values a clean head with bright hair will cover it up while sweeping. Coquettish little sweeping caps may be made by cutting a piece of bright pink, blue or gray cambric in a circular shape, and making a shirr within two inches of the edge (which should be hemmed) and running in an elastic or a piece of narrow tape with which it can be drawn up to fit the head.

—Woman's Favorite Cook Book, 1907

TO WASH CORSETS

To keep a pair of corsets perfectly fresh and clean they should be washed every two or three weeks. The operation is simple and will not injure the shape or cut. Make warm suds into which a few drops of ammonia have been put. Spread the corset on a flat table, taking out the laces but not the bones and steels. Scrub it with a clean brush and the hot suds, then rinse quickly in clear warm water. Lay flat on a board in the sun or near the fire so that they may dry quickly.

—Woman's Favorite Cook Book, 1907

Nanaimo Bars

How many Chambers of Commerce mail out recipes? The Nanaimo, British Columbia, Tourist and Convention Bureau regularly mails out the recipe for "Nanaimo Bars" in response to requests. It seems that some 35 years ago a Nanaimo woman won a recipe contest with some luscious three-layer bars. Before long everyone in the area was making them, but with more and more variations. A couple of years ago the mayor of Nanaimo decided to hold another contest to determine the real, official recipe. A winner was picked, and that's the recipe now mailed out to calorie-scorning cooks all over the country.

But some time during those 35 years the recipe reached Minnesota. It appears in *My Favorite Recipes*, put out in 1962 by Augustana Lutheran Church Women of Immanuel Lutheran Church in Almelund, Minnesota. Only there they're called "Prayer Bars," and were contributed by Mrs. Ellis Sedlund.

Prayer Bars

First layer:
½ cup butter
4 T cocoa
1 egg, beaten
1 tsp vanilla
2 cups coconut
½ cup nuts
2 cups graham cracker crumbs
½ cup powdered sugar
Second layer:
¼ cup butter, melted
2 tsp vanilla

2 T cream
2 T vanilla pudding powder
2 cups powdered sugar

Melt butter, cocoa, egg and vanilla in double boiler. Bring to boil (over boiling water), then add coconut, nuts, graham cracker crumbs and powdered sugar. Mix well, chill, then press into 9 by 13-inch pan.

Cook butter, vanilla, cream and pudding mix for one minute. Add powdered sugar, mix and spread over first layer. Chill.

Melt one 9½ ounce sweet chocolate bar and spread on top. Chill. Cut in squares.

(The Nanaimo recipe calls for a quarter cup less crumbs and a half cup butter in the second layer. For the top layer it suggests melting four squares of semisweet chocolate with two tablespoons unsalted butter.)

Pineapple Coconut Bars

1 cup brown sugar, firmly packed
¼ cup butter or margarine
1 cup sifted flour
½ tsp salt
1½ cups shredded coconut

Cream well and press half of mixture firmly into a greased 9″ square pan. Spread following pineapple filling evenly over surface.

Filling:
¾ cup granulated sugar
3 T cornstarch
¼ tsp salt
1 cup crushed pineapple, not drained
1 T lemon juice
1 T butter

Mix first 4 ingredients, bring to a boil. Cook until thick. Add lemon juice and butter. Cool slightly. Spread onto first layer and then cover with remaining crumbs and press top firmly. Bake at 350° for 35 minutes.

Molasses Bars

½ cup shortening
½ cup sugar
1 egg
½ cup molasses
½ tsp cloves
⅓ cup strong hot coffee
1½ cup flour
1½ tsp baking powder
¼ tsp soda
1 tsp cinnamon
½ tsp salt
1 cup raisins

Mix. Pour in oiled pan and bake at 350°. Frost and cut in squares.

Fruit Cake Bar

1½ cups brown sugar, packed
2 eggs, beaten
2 T cream
¾ cup butter
1 cup candied fruit, chopped
1 cup raisins
1 cup currants
2 cups flour
1 tsp soda
¼ tsp salt
½ tsp nutmeg
½ tsp cinnamon
1 cup chopped nuts

Sift together flour, salt and spices. Cream butter and brown sugar thoroughly, add eggs. Beat until fluffy. Stir in cream and sifted dry ingredients. Fold in fruits and nuts. Spread evenly in greased 15½″ × 10½″ pan. Bake in slow oven (300°) for 45 to 50 minutes. Cool in pan on cake rack. Cut in bars or diamond shapes. Dust with powdered sugar or leave plain.

Hello Dolly *or* 7-Layer Bar

Melt in 9 × 13 pan, 1 stick butter. Crush 1 individual pack of graham crackers and sprinkle over melted butter. Sprinkle over this ½ cup chopped walnut meats. Add 1 package chocolate chips and 1 package butterscotch chips over nutmeats and 1 cup of coconut over the chips. Pour one can sweetened condensed milk over top. Bake 25 minutes or until golden brown at 350°. 8 × 12 pan.

Layer Bars

First layer:
½ cup butter
¼ cup sugar
1 egg
5 T cocoa
1 cup coconut
¼ cup nutmeats
2 cups graham cracker crumbs

Cream butter and sugar. Add rest of ingredients and cook over low heat. Keep stirring until butter is melted. Mix in coconut, nutmeats and graham cracker crumbs.

Pat in cake pan, 7 × 11, and put in refrigerator.

Second layer:
3 T evaporated milk
2 cups powdered sugar

Mix and spread over chilled first layer.

Third layer:
1 6-oz pkg chocolate chips
1 T butter

Melt in double boiler and stir until smooth. Spread over second layer. Chill.

Dream Bars

½ cup butter (scant)
2 eggs, beaten
1 cup coconut
½ cup walnuts
½ cup brown sugar
1 cup sifted pastry flour

Mix and put into an 8 × 8 pan and bake until brown.

1 cup brown sugar
2 eggs
2 T flour
1 tsp baking powder
1 tsp vanilla

Cut into pieces while hot.

Matrimonial Bars

(This recipe, with very few variations, can be found in almost every church cookbook put out after 1920. Where did the name come from?)

½ pkg pitted dates
½ cup brown sugar
1 cup water
⅛ tsp salt

Bring to a boil. Cool and add 1 teaspoon vanilla and a small piece of butter.

Mix:

2 cups oatmeal
1 cup shortening
2 cups flour
1 tsp salt

Mix like pie crust. Divide crumbs. Put half in a buttered 10 × 10 × 2 pan. Add date filling, then remaining crumbs. Bake in moderate oven.

Caramel Brickle Bars

1½ cups sifted flour
¾ cup brown sugar
½ cup butter
½ tsp salt

Mix like pie crust. Put in greased 13″ × 9″ pan. Bake at 350° 10 minutes. Cool.

Brickle:

1 6-oz pkg caramel chips
2 T butter
1 cup nuts (mixed salted or cashews)
½ cup white corn syrup
1 T water

Combine all but nuts and stir until melted and smooth. Spoon this over baked crust and put nuts on top. Bake at 350° for 10 to 15 minutes. Cool to lukewarm and cut into bars.

Lemon Squares

1½ cups flour
½ cup brown sugar
½ cup butter

Mix and pat in flat pan. Bake 10 minutes at 250–275°.

Filling:

1 cup brown sugar
1½ cups coconut
1 cup nuts
2 eggs, well beaten
½ tsp baking powder
¼ tsp salt
½ tsp vanilla
2 T flour

Beat eggs. Add sugar, flour, baking powder, and rest. Spread on first mixture, and bake in a very slow oven 20 minutes. Frost with powdered sugar and lemon juice icing.

Lemon Squares

1 cup flour
½ cup butter (softened)
¼ cup confectioners' sugar
2 eggs
1 cup granulated sugar
½ tsp baking powder
¼ tsp salt
2 T lemon juice

Heat oven to 350°. Cream flour, butter and confectioners' sugar. Press evenly into bottom of ungreased square 9 × 9 × 2-inch or 8 × 8 × 2-inch pan. Bake for 20 minutes. Beat remaining ingredients until light and fluffy, about 3 minutes. Pour over hot crust and bake about 25 minutes longer or until no imprint remains when touched lightly in center. Cool and cut into 2-inch squares.

Date Orange Slice Bars

½ lb chopped dates
¼ cup sugar
½ cup boiling water
2 T flour
½ pkg candy orange slices (cut up)
1 cup brown sugar
¾ cup butter
2 eggs
1 tsp soda in 3 tsp hot water
1 tsp salt
1 tsp vanilla
1¾ cups flour

Cook dates with sugar, flour and water until tender. Add orange slices and cool. Cream sugar, butter; add eggs and soda in hot water. Add vanilla. Stir in flour and salt. Spread half of dough in 9 × 13 inch greased pan. Spread fruit mixture over this and cover with rest of dough. Bake at 350° for about 30 minutes. Cut away from sides of pan and cut into bars.

Oatmeal Filled Cookies

1 cup butter
1 cup brown sugar
2½ cups rolled oats
2½ cups flour
1 tsp soda
½ cup warm water
½ tsp vanilla

Cream sugar and butter together. Add rolled oats and flour sifted with soda. Add hot water and mix well. Roll thin on well-floured board and cut.

Filling:
⅔ lb raisins or dates
⅔ cup sugar
¾ cup water
1 level T flour
Vanilla

Mix sugar and flour together, add to raisins and water. Cook until thick. Cool before using. Add vanilla. Place small spoon filling on half the cookie, fold over and pinch edges together.

This "MONEY-BACK" Guarantee Protects You

SEAL OF MINNESOTA Flour is guaranteed to make more loaves of better bread than you can get with other flours —or you get YOUR MONEY BACK PLUS 10%.

International Milling Company

"I gotta order
SEAL OF MINNESOTA FLOUR
SOLD BY ALL WILLMAR GROCERS

Butter Scotch Sticks

¼ cup butter
1 cup brown sugar
1 egg
¼ cup broken nutmeats
1 cup sifted flour
¼ tsp salt
1 tsp baking powder
1 tsp vanilla

Melt butter in pan, add sugar, and when well-blended remove from heat and cool until lukewarm. Add unbeaten egg to mixture and beat well. Mix flour, salt and baking powder and add to sugar mixture. Then add nutmeats and vanilla. Spread in shallow pan lined with greased paper. Bake in hot oven (400–450°) till firm. While hot cut in inch strips about 4 inches long. Makes about 2 dozen.

Swedish Doughnuts

4½ cups flour
4 tsp baking powder
½ tsp nutmeg
½ tsp soda
1 tsp salt
3 eggs, beaten
1 cup sugar
1 cup mashed potatoes
2 T shortening, melted
¾ cup sour milk
½ tsp vanilla

Sift flour, measure and sift again, with baking powder, nutmeg, soda and salt. Beat eggs until light, add sugar, potatoes, melted shortening, sour milk and vanilla. Combine the two mixtures. Roll on a lightly floured board. Cut and fry as any doughnuts.

Marian Thompson remembers Saturday afternoons when she and sister Angie joined their father, who helped out as church custodian, in cleaning the church. "It meant being able to play on the organ while we dusted it. But the best part was dusting the pews. We'd sit at one end of the pew and scoot to the other end, pew after pew!"

German Doughnuts

One pint of milk, 4 eggs, 1 small tablespoonful of melted butter, flavoring, salt to taste; first boil the milk and pour it, while hot, over a pint of flour; beat it very smooth, and when it is cool, have ready the yolks of the eggs well beaten; add them to the milk and flour, beaten well into it, then add the well-beaten whites, then lastly add the salt and as much more flour as will make the whole into a soft dough; flour your board, turn your dough upon it, roll it in pieces as thick as your finger and turn them in the form of a ring; cook in plenty of boiling lard. A nice breakfast cake with coffee.

Doughnuts in Rhyme

1 cup sugar, 1 cup milk
2 eggs beaten fine as silk
Salt & nutmeg, lemon'll do
Of baking powder, teaspoons 2.
Lightly stir the 4 cups flour in.
Roll on pie board, not too thin.
Cut in diamonds, twists or rings.
Drop with care, the doughy things
Into fat that briskly swells,
Evenly the spongy cells.
Watch with care the time for turning.
Fry them brown, just short of burning.
Roll in sugar; serve when cool.
    Mrs. Ernest Krohn
    Martha Guild
    St. John's Lutheran Church
    Howard Lake, Minnesota

Pastor and Pastorska

From the time the ministers of the gospel first came from the north countries to serve frontier settlements, they were given honorary status. Even those of later date were respected for exemplifying the virtues about which they preached.

Bernhard Hillila has captured the feeling beautifully in these poems which originally appeared in the annual, "Finnish Americana," and which are reproduced here by permission. He writes of the Finnish pastor and "pastorska," but he might have been writing of almost any of the Nordic communities' spiritual leaders.

Pastor Korpi 1936

Pastor Mikko Korpi had never had an identity crisis.
He knew he wasn't Polish or Italian, and, though he spoke some Svenska, he
    most surely wasn't Swedish;
but what he wasn't most emphatically was Russian — oh, and Irish:
he was Finnish.
Fair-skinned, blue-eyed, his only relation to other races was a missionary zeal.

More pertinent to his pastoring, he was Finnish Lutheran. (Lutheran Finnish is
    redundant.)
Norwegian Lutherans and German Lutherans were brothers,
Methodists and Congregationalists at least half-brothers;
Baptists needed correction, Catholics reformation, others Christ's salvation.

Of course, there were Finnish Lutherans and there were Finnish Lutherans;
He had been trained at Suomi Theological Seminary,
and he was pastor in The Finnish Evangelical Lutheran Church of America (The
    Suomi Synod)
true daughter church of the Church of Finland,
not adherent to a sect like the Laestadians who called their loose-knit group The
    Finnish Apostolic Lutheran Church of America, or like the Evangelicals who
    called themselves The Finnish Evangelical Lutheran National Church.

Among his fellow pastors Korpi seemed high church —
he wore his clergy collar even to the hardware store.
He was strictly orthodox when preaching in his black Prince Albert and white
    collar bands —
if someone harbored doubts about the Trinity, the Resurrection,
he quoted them much Scripture, and concluded, "God's ways are not our ways."
He was quite pietistic in his own style of life —
kalja was his hardest beverage, his wife could wear no rouge.
He made it clear he didn't approve of the "hall Finns" who danced at the Finnish
    Hall, played cards and put on plays of questionable morality.

Although to sociologists a "marginal man," he somehow wasn't lost between the
    old country and the new,
but saw himself a bridge from generation to generation, culture to culture.
Instead of wondering whether he was Finnish or American, he knew that he was
    both, and the hyphen didn't bother him.
He labored hard at speaking English, exploding the k's and p's and t's becoming
    more familiar with those strange sounds in *why* and *think* and *sing*.
He started English services
    an English-speaking Luther League,
    an English choir
    ("If our young people marry other-speaking, are we going to lose them to the
        other churches?")
even though old Mikkola grumbled at Church Council,
"Before long they'll want English at the Council meetings and at the annual
    congregational meeting!"
But he also held a Finnish summer school so children and grandchildren would
    read and write in Finnish.

Beneath his clergy collar and authority, he was a tender man,
often moved to tears when visiting Mrs. Peltomaa, whose husband died in the
    mine, or hearing Saturday confession before the bi-monthly communion or
    while preaching God's love with a touching illustration
(quite different from Pastor Paakki in the neighboring parish who got angry when
    he preached.)

Pastor Korpi had accepted God when just a lad and as a corollary of God's grace,
    he had accepted Mikko Korpi.
He had never had an identity crisis.

Pastorska Anna-Liisa Korpi 1936

That was the way it was among the Finns, even American Finns —
a woman received not only the name of her husband but also his title at marriage.
Without the complications of university studies or commencement exercises,
a girl marrying a doctor became a *"tohtorinaa,"*
the wife of a *"rovasti"* (senior pastor) became a *"ruustinna."*
and a pastor's spouse was known as *"pastorska."*

Thus Anna-Kaisa Lehtonen with a simple "I do" became *pastorska* Korpi.
Yet she was always *pastorska* Anna-Kaisa Korpi, not *pastorska* Mikko Korpi —
different languages have different chauvinisms,
and that's the way it was among the Finns.
But she was *pastorska* with a lower case "p," as is tha case whenever Finns use
    titles, from "mrs" to *"presidentti"*
different languages have different usages,
and that's the way it was among the Finns.

The title really was appropriate, for everyone assumed
she'd be an unpaid pastoral assistant, active in the Ladies' Aid leading
    deaconesses in their calls, singing in the choir, teaching Sunday School,
    hostessing all visiting preachers and countless committee meetings, unlocking
    the neighboring church doors for those whose turn it was to clean for Sunday,
    taking calls for Pastor, when he was elsewhere in his four-point parish,
all in addition, of course, to keeping an immaculate house and bringing up the
    children as models for the congregation.

She was well qualified — from a good farm family, a graduate of Suomi Junior
    College, fluent in Finnish and English, blessed with a strong contralto, and
    noted for her piety.

She had her compensations — she and Pastor were seated first at the coffee table
    after midweek service, after Ladies' Aid, after choir rehearsal, after funerals.
She took some pride in knowing that the mayor, mining company bosses and the
    school "supi" contacted Pastor Korpi as a leader of the Finnish community
    when they had special concerns.
Besides, she had several fine hats and a fur piece,
and among the Finns she was called *"pastorska."*

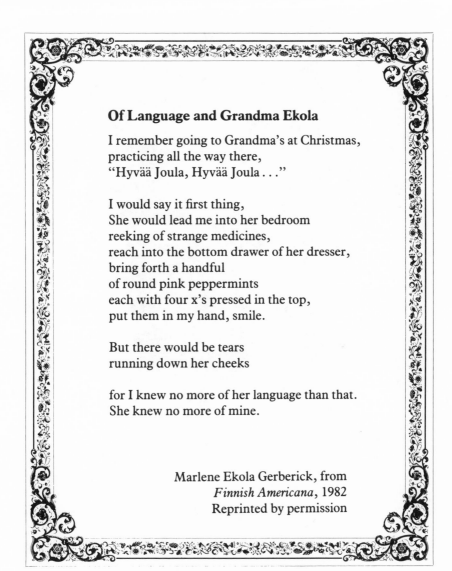

Of Language and Grandma Ekola

I remember going to Grandma's at Christmas,
practicing all the way there,
"Hyvää Joula, Hyvää Joula..."

I would say it first thing,
She would lead me into her bedroom
reeking of strange medicines,
reach into the bottom drawer of her dresser,
bring forth a handful
of round pink peppermints
each with four x's pressed in the top,
put them in my hand, smile.

But there would be tears
running down her cheeks

for I knew no more of her language than that.
She knew no more of mine.

Marlene Ekola Gerberick, from
Finnish Americana, 1982
Reprinted by permission

Cakes

In the early 1950s a distant relative of my husband's stopped to visit us on her way from a trip to the West Coast. With her she brought a discovery she had found in the big city: a box of packaged angel food cake mix.

I was frankly (and, I'm afraid, outspokenly) skeptical. My own angel foods made with an electric mixer were enough of a departure: my mother had measured her egg whites into an immense deep platter and beaten them to stiff peaks with a wire beater.

But Hulda proceeded to demonstrate and in minutes the cake was rising to amazing heights in the oven. Tasting it, I was a convert.

But if you've never made an angel food "from scratch," try it at least once, just to experience the moist, delicate, melt-in-the-mouth texture that gave the cake its name.

In the 1940s cookbook of the Willing Workers Class of the Church of the Brethren in Morrill, Kansas, is an angel food recipe. When I read these words among the directions, "Raise the pan above the table 12 inches and drop. Repeat," I knew it had to be included here! It's a wonderful recipe and says everything.

We've left Mrs. Homer Ross's directions as they were in the Willing Workers' book. Using a measuring cup instead of her peanut butter glass, you'll have the same proportions and still a good-sized cake. And be thankful for your electric mixer.

Angel Food Cake

1½ glass pure cane sugar
1½ glass chilled egg whites
Pinch salt
Flavoring
1 glass cake flour
1 slightly rounded tsp cream tartar
(Glass is large sized peanut butter glass
    holding about 1½ cups)

Use large bell shaped enamel bowl or crock. Pour in the eggs and pinch salt and with a wire spoon beater begin to beat until they turn white. Then add cream of tartar. Beat until they form a point when beater is lifted. Then begin to add sugar in small quantities, perhaps 10 to 12 portions. Next add flour from the sifter in the same quantities but stirring in with cake spoon rather than beater. And last add the flavoring. Pour in angel food pan that has been rubbed with flour. Raise the pan above the table 12 inches, and drop.

Repeat. This process settles the batter, makes the cake finer grained, and not large holes and coarse texture so often found.

Bake from 50 minutes to 1 hour. Have oven warm when cake is first put in and keep about the same temperature for the first 20 minutes. I test cake by gently placing finger on the top, if it does not leave an impression the cake is done. Remove, turn upside down and when perfectly cold, loosen by carefully running a knife around the pan and shake out.

Sift the flour only twice, once into the measure and once from the sifter into the cake. Sugar, I do not sift at all. Over-sifting incorporates too much air and causes the cake to become coarse and full of holes.

Angel Food Yellow Cake

Yolks 12 eggs
2 cups sugar
1 cup boiling water
3 cups flour
4 tsp baking powder
2 tsp lemon extract
1 small tsp salt

Use wire egg whip and beat the eggs, then add sugar and beat very hard. Then add the boiling water and beat for about 10 minutes or until it is quite thick and creamy. Then add flour, baking powder and salt sifted together. Bake in a pan same as angel food. Do not grease pan. Turn pan over same as you do in the white angel food cake.

Yellow Angel Cake

5 eggs
½ cup cold water
1¼ cups sugar
1½ cups sifted flour
2 tsp baking powder
½ tsp salt
¾ tsp cream of tartar
1 tsp vanilla
1 tsp lemon extract

Beat eggs and water together until very light and fluffy. Fold in sugar. Sift the flour, baking powder and salt together and fold in to the previous mixture. Add cream of tartar and flavoring last. Bake in a 350° oven for 35 to 40 minutes.

Yellow and White Angel Food

Beat until stiff but not dry, 1½ cups egg whites, about 9 to 11 eggs, add ½ teaspoon salt and 1 teaspoon cream of tartar. When beaten foamy, fold in 1¼ cups sugar. Divide this mixture in two parts. To one part carefully fold in ½ cup cake flour sifted 5 times and ½ teaspoon vanilla. Fold the other half of the egg whites into 6 unbeaten yellows and ⅔ cup flour sifted 5 times and ½ teaspoon lemon or orange extract. Put by spoonfuls into ungreased angel food cake pan and alternate yellow and white as in marble cake. Bake 60 minutes in slow oven.

Mock Angel Food Cake

2 cups cake flour
2 cups sugar

Sift together until well mixed, put in mixing bowl. 1 cup hot water over this, mix whites of 5 eggs beaten stiff. 2 teaspoons baking powder in whites of eggs when half beaten. Mix beaten egg whites with sugar and flour and ½ teaspoon vanilla. Bake in slow oven ½ hour or 45 minutes.

Sunshine Cake

7 egg whites
1 tsp cream of tartar
1¼ cups sugar
5 egg yolks
1 cup flour
1 tsp vanilla

Sift flour and sugar 3 or 4 times separately. Beat egg whites stiff and add cream of tartar. Fold in sugar gradually, then beaten egg yolks. Lastly fold in flour and add vanilla. Bake in cold oven (250°) for half an hour. Increase 25° for 15 minutes. Increase another 25° for another 15 minutes.

Lady Baltimore Cake

1 cup sugar
⅓ cup butter
3 egg whites
1½ cups flour
2 tsp baking powder
¾ cup milk

Cream butter, add sugar. Cream well. Add alternately sifted flour and baking powder, and milk. Beat well. Add beaten whites of eggs. Pour in buttered pan, and bake in loaf 30 minutes in moderate oven, or in layers 20 minutes.

Frosting:

Beat yolk of one egg. Add one tablespoon melted butter and one tablespoon milk. Stir in powdered sugar to right consistency. Flavor with vanilla or maple flavoring.

White Cake — Lover's Dream

1½ cups sugar
½ cup butter (scant — creamed well)
½ cup water (scant)
2 cups cake flour (measure before sifting)
1 tsp baking powder
5 egg whites

Cream butter well, add sugar gradually, sift flour and baking powder, add alternately with water. Flavor, and add egg whites beaten stiff.

Lazy Daisy Cake

2 eggs, beaten until thick
1 cup of sugar added gradually to eggs, beating constantly
Add 1 tsp vanilla
1 cup pastry flour measured after sifting

Add to flour 1 tsp baking powder and ¼ tsp salt. Sift once more and add to eggs and sugar mixture.

½ cup milk (heat to boiling point)
1 T butter (add to hot milk)

Mix all together, beating well. Bake in 8″ square pan ½ hour at 375°.

Topping:

3 T melted butter
5 T brown sugar
2 T cream
½ cup coconut

Mix all together and spread on cake after it is baked. Put under broiler for two or three minutes watching carefully. When it bubbles and is slightly brown it is done.

Never Fail Jelly Roll

4 eggs, beaten until very light
1 T cold water
1 cup sugar
1 tsp vanilla
1 cup flour sifted with 2 tsp phosphate baking powder

Mix in the order given and pour into a pan about 9 × 20 inches. Bake in a moderate oven for about twenty minutes. Turn out while hot, spread with jelly and roll at once. Three rules to remember for a successful jelly roll are these:

1. Beat the eggs thoroughly.
2. Bake the cake in a moderate oven (325–350°).
3. Roll while hot.

Jelly Roll Cake

1 cup sugar
4 eggs
3 T sweet milk
1 cup flour
1 tsp baking powder
1 tsp vanilla
1 pinch salt

Beat eggs till very light, add sugar and beat well. Sift baking powder, flour, salt, three times. Add alternately with milk. Bake in moderate oven. When done turn upside down on a wet cloth or a cloth spread with powdered sugar. Spread with jelly and roll while warm. Sprinkle with powdered sugar.

Sweet Cream Cake

1 cup sugar
1½ cup flour
3 level tsp baking powder

Sift together then add:

1 cup sweet cream
2 eggs
1 tsp vanilla

Beat well. For variety one can add cocoa, spices, or burnt sugar to taste.

Sour Cream Cake

2 eggs
½ cup sugar
½ cup corn syrup
¾ cups thick, sour cream
⅔ tsp soda
½ tsp vanilla
2 cups cake flour
2 tsp baking powder
1 tsp salt

Beat eggs. Add sugar, corn syrup, cream, and soda. Combine well. Add vanilla. Add sifted dry ingredients, and bake in loaf pan at 350° for 45 minutes, or in 2 8-inch pans at 375° for 25 minutes.

$100 Cake

1 cup mayonnaise or salad dressing
1 cup sugar
2 tsp soda
4 T cocoa
1 cup cold water
2 cups enriched flour
½ tsp salt

Mix sugar, cocoa; add mayonnaise. Sift flour, soda, salt and add to mayonnaise mixture alternately with water. Beat thoroughly. Bake at 350° in two 8-inch layer or loaf pan for 25 to 35 minutes.

Whipped Cream Cake

1 cup sweet cream whipped
1 cup sugar
1½ cups cake flour, sifted 3 times
2 tsp baking powder
1 tsp vanilla
½ tsp salt
2 eggs

Whip cream until stiff. Drop in eggs and whip till very light. Add sugar and beat again. Add vanilla and fold in dry ingredients very slowly and bake in layer cake tins in a moderately hot oven. Very feathery and delicious. Frost with any favorite frosting.

Snow Balls

1 cup white sugar
1 cup thick cream
5 whites of egg
3 tsp baking powder
½ tsp almond flavoring or any preferred
    flavoring
2 cups flour

Sift dry ingredients, add cream and fold in stiffly beaten egg whites and add flavoring. Bake in small well greased pans (use muffin tins with cupcake liners) and cover with a plain white icing when cool.

Lemonade Cake

2 cups flour
2 tsp baking powder
¼ tsp salt
1 cup milk, scalded
4 eggs
2 cups sugar
6 oz can frozen lemonade concentrate,
    thawed
2 T butter

Sift flour, baking powder and salt. Beat eggs until light. Beat in sugar, 1 tablespoon lemonade concentrate, milk and butter. Blend in dry ingredients. Pour batter in 9 × 13 pan. Bake at 350° for 30 to 35 minutes. Cool, cut and serve with warm topping.

Topping:

1 cup sugar
3 T flour
2 eggs
2 T butter
¼ tsp salt

Remainder of lemonade concentrate. Combine all ingredients in heavy sauce pan, cook over medium heat until mixture thickens and bubbles.

The Tolling

"I might be out in a field setting traps for gophers—the farmers paid five cents for the tail of a striped gopher and ten cents for a pocket gopher—or playing near our parsonage, which was less than a block from our country church. But I'd hear the bell begin to toll, and there was that startling awareness that someone in the church family had died, and I'd wonder, 'Who?' "

Paul Seastrand, son of a rural pastor and himself a retired pastor of churches in Washington, Texas, Montana and Minnesota, was talking about a custom in the old Augustana (Swedish) Lutheran churches.

"As soon as the pastor learned of the death of a member, he'd call the custodian to toll the big bell in the church steeple, very slowly, and often one toll for each year of the person's life.

"Then there was the funeral, which started with a service at home, where the casket of the deceased had been brought. Sometimes the house would be filled all the way to the kitchen, with the crowd spilling over outside. Meanwhile the church custodian would have climbed the ladder to the bell tower, where he could look out at roads coming from three directions. As soon as the hearse and slow procession of cars was in sight, he would begin again the slow tolling of the bell, several seconds between each strike. The tolling ended only when the casket had been borne into the church.

"Finally, the service over, the bell would again toll as the procession made its slow way to the cemetery just back of the church.

"Solemn? Yes. But it was a message to hear and respond to."

According to Lenus Ekstrand, who helped his father ring the bell at the North Crow River Church in Minnesota, the bell was not actually "rung" for a funeral. Instead of being pulled with a rope, the bell was struck with a foot-operated hammer-like apparatus that was fastened to a platform next to the bell. This made the slow tolling possible.

The slow tolling was used at one other time—the New Year's Eve Watch Night Service. At a few minutes before midnight it would begin a slow ringing out of the old year, but when the hands of the clock passed twelve the bell broke into a vigorous ringing in of the new year.

Fudge Cake

1½ cups sugar
½ cup shortening
2 eggs
½ cup cocoa
⅓ cup hot water
½ cup sour milk
2¼ cups flour
1 tsp soda
1 tsp baking powder
½ tsp salt
1 tsp vanilla

Pour hot water over cocoa. Let cool.
Cream shortening and sugar, add egg yolks
and beat. Add cooled cocoa mixture. Sift
dry ingredients together and add
alternately with sour milk. Add flavoring
and beaten egg whites. Bake in moderate
oven.

Sour Cream Chocolate Cake

½ cup cocoa
½ tsp soda
½ cup boiling water
2 eggs
1½ cups sugar
2 cups sifted cake flour
½ tsp salt
1 cup thick sour cream

Mix together cocoa, soda and boiling
water. Let cool. Beat eggs well and add
sugar, beating until light in color. Add
sifted ingredients alternately with sour
cream. Add cocoa mixture. Pour in 9 × 12
pan. Bake in 350° oven for 30 to 45
minutes.

Never Fail Devil's Food Cake

¾ cup butter
⅓ cup cocoa
2 cups sugar
1 cup sour milk
1 tsp soda
2½ cups flour
1 tsp baking powder
1 tsp flavoring
3 eggs
1 cup nuts, if desired

Cream butter and gradually add sugar.
Continue the creaming until the sugar
granules dissolve. Separate the eggs and
beat the yolks until light colored. Add to
the butter and sugar mixture and beat well.
Dissolve the soda in the milk and add
alternately the flour mixed with the baking
powder.

Dissolve the soda in as little water as
possible and add to the cake batter. Add
the nuts and fold in the stiffly beaten egg
whites and then add the vanilla extract.
Bake in a moderate oven.

Potato Caramel Cake

2 cups sugar
1 cup butter
4 eggs
½ cup milk
1 cup mashed potatoes
1 cup cocoa
1 cup nuts
2 cups flour
2 T baking powder

Cream butter and sugar thoroughly. Add
beaten yolks, mashed potatoes, nuts. Sift
flour and baking powder and add
alternately with the milk. Last fold in
stiffly beaten whites and bake in layers in a
moderate oven.

Prince of Wales Cake

*This, and Prince of Wales Pudding, appears
in several older books.*

1 cup sugar
½ cup butter
2 eggs
½ cup sour milk
½ tsp soda
½ tsp cloves
1 tsp cinnamon
1 tsp baking powder
½ tsp nutmeg
1 T molasses
1½ cups flour

Mix in order given.

A former owner of a cookbook from Elk Creek and Chimney Rock parishes in Wisconsin had crossed out the title of this recipe, "Hill Billy Cake," and had written in "Threshers' Cake" instead:

Threshers' Cake

1 cup sugar
1 cup raisins
1 cup cold water
½ cup butter
½ cup nutmeats
½ tsp salt
¼ tsp cloves
¼ tsp allspice
½ tsp cinnamon

Combine together and boil for one minute. Let cool; add the following: 2 cups flour with 2 teaspoons soda. Bake 30 minutes in 350° oven.

"Brown Stone Front" cake recipes are found in many old cookbooks. The origin? Could it have been from the years when the brownstone fronts of New York and Chicago housed "up and coming" families with cooks and parlor maids who ate cakes not quite as fancy as those served the family?

Brown Stone Front

2 cups brown sugar
½ cup butter
Pinch salt
1 cup sour milk
1 tsp soda
1 tsp cinnamon
½ tsp cloves, allspice and nutmeg
2½ cups flour
1 cup raisins
½ cup chopped walnuts
3 egg whites, stiffly beaten

Mix in order given. Ice with chocolate.

Brown Stone Front

1½ cups sugar
¼ cup butter
3 eggs
1 cup sour cream
1 pinch salt
1 tsp soda
½ cup cocoa
½ cup hot water
1 tsp vanilla
2 cups flour

Beat eggs in separately. Add soda in cream. Makes 3 layers or a loaf.

Wyoming Cake

⅔ cup butter
1 cup brown sugar
½ cup molasses (light)
2 eggs
1 cup sour milk
½ cup nutmeats
2 tsp soda
2½ cups flour
1½ tsp cinnamon
½ tsp cloves
1½ cups raisins

Bake in oven 350° for 40 minutes.

Oatmeal Cake

1½ cups boiling water
1 cup quick oatmeal
1 cup brown sugar
1 cup white sugar
½ cup shortening or butter
2 beaten eggs
1½ cups flour
1 tsp soda
1 tsp baking powder
1 tsp cinnamon
½ tsp salt
1 tsp vanilla

Pour boiling water over the oatmeal. Mix brown and white sugar, shortening well and add beaten eggs. Sift all dry ingredients together and add to mixture and add vanilla. Bake at 350° for 35−45 minutes in 9 × 13″ pan. Top with following topping. Broiled.

1 cup brown sugar
¼ cup oleo or butter
¼ cup milk
1 cup flaked coconut

Mix and spread on cake and broil 2−3 minutes at 250°.

Showers of Blessing

How many uses the church basement had! Not only the usual church serving, but wedding receptions, funeral lunches, anniversary parties, and those high-church occasions when the whole district would gather for "Mission Meeting," a dozen or more pastors in their square black coats and "*prästa kraga,*" delegates in Sunday best, and the best cooks of the parish perspiring in the kitchen.

Wedding showers alternated between the church basement and the home. Laila Maudslien remembers well her wedding shower in Whitman, North Dakota, in June, 1942.

"I had gone to Seattle to work and met Ed, and when he learned the Navy wasn't shipping him out right away he asked me to marry him. But I wanted to go home and see my folks first, and when I got there all the people in the neighborhood had a shower for me. They hadn't seen Ed, so I brought pictures of him to show everyone."

Grandma Sigrid Lillehaugen studied the pictures.

"Well, what do you think?"

Grandma replied in Norwegian. "Those who have luck," she said, "don't need any sense."

"But Grandma, which do you think I have?"

"That," said Grandma, "we will have to wait and see."

Forty-six years later Laila and Ed allow as how they may have had some of both.

Raw Apple Cake

½ cup brown sugar
1 cup white sugar
½ cup shortening (butter preferred)
2 eggs
2 tsp cinnamon
1 cup sour milk or buttermilk
2¼ cups all purpose flour
¼ tsp salt
2 tsp soda
2 cups raw apples, sliced thin

Mix dry ingredients, shortening, and milk in a bowl. Beat 2 minutes. Add eggs and beat well. Fold in apples. Pour into greased and floured 9 × 12 pan. Pour topping over cake batter and bake for 45 minutes at 350°

Topping:

¼ cup brown sugar
¼ cup white sugar
½ tsp cinnamon
½ cup chopped nuts

Fresh Apple Cake

Cream ½ cup butter and 1 cup sugar. Add 2 eggs and beat well. Sift 1½ cup flour, 1 teaspoon soda, ¾ teaspoon ground cloves and add alternately with ½ cup cold strong coffee. Stir in 2 cups finely chopped raw apples, 1 cup raisins and ½ cup chopped nuts. Bake at 350° about 50 minutes.

Apple Sauce Cake

¼ cup shortening
¾ cup sugar
½ tsp salt
1 egg
1 cup apple sauce
1½ cups flour
1 tsp soda
½ tsp cinnamon and cloves
½ cup chopped nuts
½ cup chopped raisins
½ cup chopped dates

Blend shortening, sugar, salt and egg. Add sauce alternately with dry ingredients. Stir in nuts, raisins and dates. Bake 40 to 45 minutes.

Rhubarb Cake

1½ cups brown sugar, packed
¼ cup sugar
½ cup shortening
1 egg
1 tsp vanilla
2 cups sifted flour
1 tsp soda
1 cup buttermilk or thick sour milk
1½ cups raw, cut up rhubarb
½ tsp nutmeg
½ tsp cinnamon

Spread half of batter in a 9×3 pan, greased. Place rhubarb on top of the batter and spoon remaining batter on top.

Mix together:

⅓ cup sugar
1 tsp cinnamon

Sprinkle on top of cake and bake about 50 minutes in moderate oven.

Tomato Soup Cake

½ cup shortening
1 cup sugar
1 can tomato soup
½ tsp soda
2 cups flour
1 tsp baking powder
2 tsp nutmeg
1 tsp cinnamon
1 tsp cloves
¼ tsp salt
1 cup dates
1 cup nuts

Cream shortening and sugar; then add the soup, sifted dry ingredients, and the dates and nuts. Bake 45 minutes.

Coffee Raisin Cake

½ cup butter
1 cup brown sugar
2 eggs
2 cups flour
½ cup cold coffee
½ cup molasses
1 tsp cinnamon
1 tsp allspice
½ tsp cloves
1 cup floured raisins

Mix butter, sugar and eggs to a cream. Add rest of ingredients and bake in moderate oven in loaf pan.

Sour Cream Cake

1 egg
1 cup sugar
1 cup sour cream
1 tsp soda
2 cups flour
½ tsp cloves
½ tsp cinnamon
½ tsp nutmeg (scant)

Beat the egg, then add the sugar. Add the sour cream; sift flour and spices together and add to the above mixture. Add flavoring and bake in a square tin.

Carrot Cake

3 cups grated carrots
4 eggs, unbeaten
2 cups sugar
1½ cups salad oil
2 tsp soda
½ tsp salt
2 cups flour
1 tsp cinnamon
1 tsp vanilla
1 cup nutmeats

Combine eggs, carrots, sugar and oil. Mix well, add other ingredients. Beat well. Bake 350° for 40 to 45 minutes. (A large cake)
    Topping:

1 pkg cream cheese 8 oz
½ lb powdered sugar
½ cup butter
1 cup nutmeats (optional)

Beat until fluffy.

Pineapple Upside Down Cake

⅓ cup shortening
⅛ tsp salt
½ cup sugar
1 egg unbeaten
5 slices canned pineapple
1¼ cups sifted flour
1½ tsp baking powder
½ cup canned pineapple juice
½ cup brown sugar firmly packed

Combine shortening and salt. Add sugar and cream until fluffy. Add egg and beat thoroughly. Sift flour and baking powder three times. Add small amounts of flour to creamed mixture alternately with pineapple juice, beating until smooth. Sprinkle brown sugar on bottom of deep 8×8 inch pan greased with butter. Arrange pineapple slices on sugar and pour batter over all. Bake in moderate oven 50 to 60 minutes. Serve with whipped cream.

Most church cookbooks carried a recipe like this. Have you ever tried them? They really work!

A Scriptural Cake

1 cup Judges 5:25
2 cups Jeremiah 6:20
2½ cups 1 Kings 4:22
2 cups 1 Samuel 30:12
1 cup Numbers 17:8
1 cup Genesis 24:20
6 Isaiah 10:14
1 T Exodus 16:31
Pinch of Leviticus 2:13
2 tsp 1 Corinthians 5:6
Sweets in 1 Kings 10:2

Mix in order given and follow Solomon's Advice given in Proverbs 23:14.

Orange Cake

½ cup shortening
2 eggs (beaten)
1 tsp baking powder
½ tsp salt
1 cup sugar
2 cups flour
1 tsp salt
1 cup buttermilk

Add peel of 1 large orange and 1 cup raisins put through food chopper twice. Bake. Mix ½ cup sugar with juice of 1 large orange and pour over cake as soon as removed from oven.

Graham Cracker Cake

½ cup shortening
1 cup sugar
3 eggs
1 cup milk
23 graham crackers
¾ cup coconut
3 tsp baking powder
Pinch of salt
About 1 cup flour

Roll crackers until they crumb. Mix dry ingredients, add other materials and fold beaten egg whites in last.

White Fruit Cake

2 cups sugar
1 cup butter
1 cup milk
3½ cups cake flour
5 egg whites beaten
1 or 2 cups coconut
1 heaping tsp baking powder
2 cups white raisins
1 rind candied lemon peel
1 rind candied orange peel
1 rind candied pineapple peel
¼ pound citron
1 cup walnut meats
1 cup Brazil nuts
30 candied cherries
2 tsp vanilla

Add beaten egg whites last. Bake 1 hour or more in moderate oven. This makes a large sized cake. Line baking pan with several thicknesses of wax paper and let it extend about an inch over the edge. Put a pan of water on bottom rack in oven when baking. This gives all fruit cakes a finer texture and glazed top. Keep cake wrapped in wax paper in cool place. This cake lasts for months.

Economical Fruit Cake

3 cups brown sugar
1 cup shortening
4 eggs beaten separately
½ tsp salt
2 tsp cinnamon
1 tsp cloves
1 tsp nutmeg
½ tsp ginger
1 cup strong coffee
2 tsp soda, dissolved in coffee
1 pound currants
4 cups flour
1 cup nut meats
2 pounds raisins
1 pound dates
1 pound mixed fruits (citron, orange and lemon peel)
Figs may be added also

Cook raisins, currants, mixed fruits in enough water to cover for about 10 minutes. Cool slightly, then add dates, figs and nuts. Cream sugar, shortening, add eggs, and beat. Then add flour and spices which have been sifted together alternately with coffee, lastly add fruit, mix well. Line pans with 2 thicknesses of brown paper, grease and flour. Bake in moderate oven (300°) for 2 hours or until done. This will make two cakes. When cool wrap in waxed paper. Put away in a tin box.

Unbaked Fruit Cake

Grind:
4 cups dates
¾ cup raisins
Combine:
¾ cup candied cherries, cut in halves
1 cup candied pineapple, cubed
1½ cups chopped pecans or walnuts
¼ tsp salt
2 T orange juice

Add to first mixture and mix well with hands till a solid mass is formed. Form into roll; wrap in wax paper; refrigerate. Cut in slices to serve.

Gingerbread

2 cups flour
1½ tsp soda
½ tsp salt
1 tsp ginger
1 tsp cinnamon
½ tsp cloves
½ cup shortening
½ cup brown sugar (firmly packed)
2 eggs
¾ cups molasses
1 cup boiling water

Sift all the dry ingredients twice. Cream shortening and sugar. Add eggs and beat well. Add ¼ of the dry ingredients. Next add the molasses then the remaining dry ingredients. Add the boiling water. Bake in a moderate oven.

In 1948 Betty Crocker introduced what was called "the first new cake in 100 years, combining the best qualities of both angel food and butter cakes." The Chiffon Cake, however, appears in only a few of the 1950s cookbooks, probably because everyone already had the recipe.

Chiffon Cake

2 cups sifted flour
1½ cups sugar
3 T baking powder
½ tsp salt
½ cup salad oil
7 unbeaten egg yolks
¾ cup cold water
1 tsp vanilla
2 tsp grated lemon rind
1 cup egg whites
½ tsp cream of tartar

Sift dry ingredients into a bowl. Make a well in the center and add oil, egg yolks, water, vanilla and grated rind. Beat with spoon until smooth. Beat egg whites and cream of tartar until they form very stiff peaks. (Do NOT underbeat.) Pour yolk mixture over beaten whites, folding in just until blended. Do not stir. Pour into ungreased pan, either tube pan or 9×13 cake pan. Bake 45 to 50 minutes at 350° until top springs back when lightly touched. Turn pan upside down, edges resting on 2 other pans. Let hang until cold.

This could be frosted in any way, but a Betty Crocker book of that time suggested a frosting of 3 ounces softened cream cheese, ½ cup soft butter, 4 cups sifted confectioner's sugar, 2 T cream, 1 tsp lemon juice, 3 tsp grated lemon rind and 1 tsp vanilla, beaten until light and fluffy.

Orange Filling

1½ cup sugar
¾ cup flour
4½ T lemon juice
⅓ cup water
Rind of 1 orange

1½ cups orange juice
1 beaten egg
3 tsp butter

Combine above ingredients and cook 10 minutes stirring frequently. Spread on cake while hot and frost cake with seven minute icing. This can be served as a dessert.

Peanut Butter Filling

5 T sugar
5 egg yolks
½ cup cream
2 T peanut butter

Mix first 3 ingredients and boil until creamy (watch so as not to burn). Add the peanut butter and beat until creamy. Spread on white cake before the frosting is put on.

Filling for White Cake

Mix in saucepan:
½ cup sugar
3 T orange juice
½ cup chopped dates
1 T flour
½ cup butter

Cook over low heat. Stir until mix boils. Boil 1 minute. Pour ½ of hot mixture into 2 beaten egg yolks, stirring constantly. Add to remaining filling. Bring to a boil. Add ½ cup nuts and cool. Makes 1¼ cup.

Caramel Filling

Bake a white loaf cake and frost with thin powdered sugar frosting. Then top with the following filling:
1 T butter
1 cup brown sugar
3 T corn starch
3 egg yolks
¼ cup cream

Cook over boiling water until thick. Cool and add 1 cup broken walnuts, and spread over top of cake.

Never Fail Karo Frosting

2 egg whites
¼ cup powdered sugar
1 tsp vanilla
1 cup white Karo syrup
½ tsp salt

Put into bowl the unbeaten egg whites, syrup and salt. Beat about 10 minutes. Add powdered sugar and vanilla. Spread on cake. Sprinkle generously with coconut, chopped nuts or cherries.

Never Fail Chocolate Fudge Frosting

1 box powdered sugar
1 dash salt
5 T milk
½ tsp vanilla
2 squares chocolate
½ cup butter (¼ lb) or margarine

Melt butter and chocolate. Mix other ingredients together. Add chocolate and butter mixture. Beat until of spreading consistency.

Never Fail Chocolate Icing

2 cups powdered sugar
⅓ cup butter
2 squares melted chocolate
2 egg whites

Combine the powdered sugar and the butter and cream well. Add the melted chocolate and mix well. Add to the stiffly beaten egg whites and beat until creamy.

Strawberry Fluff Frosting

2 egg whites (unbeaten)
Dash of salt
1 cup sugar
⅔ cup strawberries (thawed and well drained)

Combine all ingredients in double boiler. Beat 1 minute. Place over boiling water. Beat until frosting forms peaks, about 7 minutes. Remove from water. Beat until spreading consistency, about 2 minutes.

Chocolate Fluff Frosting

1 cup powdered sugar
1 whole egg
¼ cup milk
½ tsp vanilla
2 squares melted chocolate
1 T butter

Place all ingredients in a bowl, set in ice or cold water. Beat with rotary beater until thick and glossy and will stand in peaks. Do not beat too long after it starts "peaking" as it thickens on cake.

Broiled Peanut Butter-Coconut Frosting

Blend:
¼ cup peanut butter
¼ cup light cream
1 cup brown sugar

Spread over warm cake (just taken from oven). Sprinkle with ½ cup flaked coconut. Broil 4 to 5 inches from heat about four minutes or until frosting is lightly browned. This frosts a 9-inch square cake generously.

Carmel Frosting

1½ cup brown sugar
2 T butter
4 T cream
1 tsp vanilla

Mix all and boil 3 or 4 minutes stirring constantly. Remove from fire and beat until creamy.

Frosting for Apple Cake

1 cup brown sugar
Pinch salt
⅓ cup cream
1 tsp vanilla

Cook sugar, cream and salt until it is thick, then test in cold water. When a drop forms a soft ball, cool and beat till it is almost thick. Add vanilla and spread.

Desserts

Lemon Is for Easter

What triggers memory for you? A snatch of a song, perhaps, or a whiff of perfume, pipe smoke drifting on night air, cinnamon spilling on toast, a certain shade of blue?

I turn the stained pages of the old cookbook and here is "Lemon Pie" with a pencilled X beside it. And immediately it is Easter, and on a round kitchen table miles in the past the scraps of the Easter ham are cooling in their congealed fat and I am cutting the lemon pie. Twice this morning we have sung, "Christ the Lord is ris'n today, Alleluiah," first on the high hill above the town, where the sunrise never quite broke through the murky cloud mass, and again with the organ sounding the triumphant news against an altar banked with lilies. We are still in our "church clothes," the resplendent white shirts, the eyelet-trimmed dresses I finished hemming at midnight.

Lemon is for Easter, cool and fresh like the morning, yellow as the pale sun beginning to break through the birch grove, yellow as the daffodils will be that are yet only hesitant shoots. We open the door, we hear the bright rush of the river almost at flood stage. The air is electric with smell of spring, alders and willows racing to be first to break into buds, pasture grass straining to life, fir and balsam across the river greeting the new warmth, and on the breeze the faint, sweet earthy smell of fertilized fields from the organic acres down the road. It's as if the whole world around us stood at the brink of life.

> "O death, where is your deadly sting?
> Al-le-lu-ia!
> Assumed by our triumphant King!
> Al-le-lu-iah!"

The well-worn book was my mother-in-law's, a 1924 edition put out by the Ladies Aid of First Lutheran Church, Sioux Falls, South Dakota. It was given her by her sister Helen Reagan of Sioux Falls. I wonder if Anna baked lemon pies on the Saturday before Easter when the Minnesota fields were waking to life. Or did she wait till summer, when her rugosa roses spilled their dark beauty outside the front door and she folded the day's wash in the coolness of the porch?

In the back of the book she has written in a recipe for lemon pie: "Grated rind of 1 lemon, squeeze out juice. ½ cup sugar, 3 egg yolks well beaten, 3 tablespoons hot water (scant), 1 teaspoon flour. Cook in double boiler till thick. Cool. 3 egg whites, beaten, add ½ cup sugar. Put in oven to brown."

This is a small tart pie that gets most of its sweetness from the meringue. Page 84 of the book looks well used, too. On it is this recipe for lemon pie: (It's the one with the X.)

Lemon Pie

1¼ cups sugar
3 T flour
Yolks of 3 eggs
Grated rind and juice of 1 lemon
1 cup cold water
Pinch of salt

Mix sugar, rind and juice, then egg yolks. Add cold water and cook 30 minutes in double boiler. Pour into baked crust and top with meringue of the 3 egg whites with 4 T sugar; brown quickly in oven.

In the same book is a torn page dated faintly, "Feb. 4, 1904," and what looks like "Minna." On it is pasted a yellowed newspaper clipping:

"Do your readers know their birthstones and birthday flowers? I will name them for those who don't: January, garnet; February, amethyst; March, bloodstone; April, diamond; May, emerald; June, agate; July, ruby; August, sardonyx; September, sapphire; October, opal; November, topaz; December, turquoise. January, wild rose; February, carnation; March, violet; April, Easter lily; May, lily of the valley; June, rose; July, daisy; August, water lily; September, poppy; October, cosmos; November, chrysanthemum; December, holly."

Lemon Cake Pudding

¾ cup sugar
2 egg yolks beaten
1 cup milk
1 T butter
2 T flour
Juice and rind of 1 lemon
2 stiffly beaten egg whites

Cream sugar and butter together, add egg yolks and blend together. Add flour and beat, add milk. When well mixed, add lemon juice, and grated rind. Fold in stiffly beaten whites of eggs and pour into slightly greased pudding dish, set in pan of hot water and bake in slow oven 325° for 50 minutes. Serves 4 persons.

Snow Pudding

1 qt milk
8 level T sugar
½ box Knox Gelatine
1 tsp vanilla
¼ cup cold water
3 eggs
¼ tsp salt

Dissolve gelatine in the cold water. Let milk and sugar come to a boil. Beat egg yolks very light, stir into the hot milk, also gelatine, boil till it bubbles. Remove from stove, add stiffly beaten whites of eggs, salt, and vanilla and mold. May be served plain or with whipped cream.

Snow Pudding (Floating Island)

Juice and rind of 1 lemon
½ cup sugar
2 rounding T corn starch
2 cups boiling water

Boil mixture until clear, then at once stir into the well beaten whites of 2 eggs. Set in cool place.

Sauce:

2 egg yolks
Sugar to taste
1 cup milk

Mix together and let simmer in double boiler until creamy. When cool, add vanilla. Scoop "islands" of first mixture into individual serving dishes and spoon custard sauce over.

Snow Balls

Mix thoroughly 4 tablespoonfuls of sugar, 4 tablespoonfuls of cornstarch, ⅛ teaspoonful of salt. Pour on slowly 1 pint of boiling water, stirring all the time. Cook directly over the fire 8 to 10 minutes, or in a double boiler 15 minutes. Remove from the stove, and add the whites of 2 eggs, beaten stiff, and the juice of ½ a lemon. Serve with a custard made of the yolks of the two eggs, 1½ cups of milk, 4 tablespoonfuls of sugar, a speck of salt, and ½ teaspoonful of vanilla.

Lemon Mold

3 eggs, beaten
1 cup sugar
juice of 1 lemon
1 cup cream

Cook in double boiler until thick. Cool. Whip 1 cup cream and fold into cold custard. Cover pan with crushed graham crackers or vanilla wafers. Place in refrigerator and cut into squares.

Old Fashioned Rice Pudding

1 cup uncooked rice
½ cup sugar
1 tsp salt
¼ cup washed raisins
1 egg
3 cups milk
Nutmeg

Wash rice, add sugar, salt and raisins. Place in baking dish. Beat egg, add milk and pour over rice. Stir together and sprinkle nutmeg over the top. Bake in 300° oven for 1½ hours. Stir two or three times while it is baking.

Bread Pudding

2 slices bread
2 beaten eggs
1 cup sugar
1 pint sweet milk
1 pint cooked raisins
1 tsp cinnamon
1 T butter

Bake slowly for 1 hour.

Bread Pudding

6 slices white bread
3 cups milk
3 eggs
2 tsp vanilla
¼ cup sugar

Beat eggs, add milk, sugar and vanilla. Break up half the bread in buttered casserole, pour over it half the liquid. Repeat. Sprinkle nutmeg or cinnamon over top. Bake in pan of hot water 30 minutes at 350°, or till set in center.

Orange Cream Pudding

½ cup orange juice
½ lb marshmallows
½ pint whipping cream

Melt marshmallows in double boiler. Add orange juice, let cool and set. Add whipped cream and put in icebox to set.

Glorified Rice

1½ cup cooked rice (cooled)
1 pkg lemon jello (prepare in usual way
 but use only 1½ cups water)
Prepare and whip:
1 cup cream (whipped)
¼ cup sugar
1 tsp vanilla

Mix rice, partially set jello and whipped cream mixture together. Refrigerate. Drained fruit cocktail, crushed pineapple, marshmallows may be added.

Heavenly Rice

Very popular in the 1930s.

2 cups cooked rice
1 cup drained pineapple
½ cup nuts
⅓ cup sugar
12 to 16 marshmallows, cut up
1 cup cream, whipped
Chopped maraschino cherries, or whole
 cherries for topping

Fold all together. Chill at least two hours.

Caramel Dumplings

Brown 1 cup sugar
Add ½ cup milk
2½ cups water
1 T butter
Pinch of salt
1 tsp vanilla

Boil until all is dissolved. Make a batter of the following:

½ cup sugar
1 T butter
½ cup milk
1 tsp baking powder
Pinch of salt
1 tsp vanilla
Flour to make batter that will drop from
spoon.

Drop small spoonfuls into hot syrup and bake in a quick oven 15 or 20 minutes.

There were many date recipes in books from the '20s and '30s.

Date Pudding

1¼ cups dates (chopped fine)
1 cup nuts
1 cup sugar
½ cup hot water
½ cup sifted flour
1 heaping tsp baking powder
3 eggs

Beat yolks of eggs light. Add sugar and beat well. Pour hot water on dates and add egg mixture and nuts. Add flour and baking powder and fold in egg whites last. Bake 35 minutes at 300°.

Date Bars

2 lbs graham crackers
2 lbs seeded dates
1 lb marshmallows

Grind crackers and dates, dice marshmallows and mix with pint of thick sweet cream. Mold into loaf (I pack this in my pound butter cartons) then slice it and serve with whipped cream.

Texas Pudding

1 cup flour
½ cup sugar
2 tsp baking powder
½ tsp nutmeg and cinnamon
Pinch of salt

Sift together, then add ½ can milk, a T melted butter and ½ cup raisins. Put in greased pan and pour over 1 cup brown sugar dissolved in 2 cups boiling water. Bake in rather hot oven. Dates may be used instead of raisins and nuts added if you like.

Carrot Pudding

½ cup shortening
½ cup brown sugar
1 egg
1¼ cups flour
½ tsp soda
1 T water
½ tsp salt
2 tsp cut lemon peel
1 cup grated raw carrots
½ cup seedless raisins
½ cup currants
1 tsp baking powder
½ tsp cinnamon
½ tsp nutmeg

Blend shortening, sugar, and eggs. Add grated carrots, raisins, currants and lemon peel. Add the sifted flour, baking powder, salt and spices. Mix thoroughly. Then add the soda dissolved in water. Cook in well greased double boiler on top of stove for 1 hour. Remove from over boiling water and bake uncovered for 20 minutes in moderate oven. Serve with pudding sauce or whipped cream. Serves 6.

Carrot Pudding

Sift:

2 cups flour
1 tsp soda
1 tsp cinnamon
1 tsp nutmeg
½ tsp salt

Add:

1 cup sugar
1 cup suet chopped
1 cup raw carrots chopped
1 cup raw potatoes chopped
1 cup raisins chopped
Dates and nuts if desired

Mix all these ingredients with the hands. Put in pound coffee tins and steam 2 hours. Serve with the following sauce:

1 egg
½ cup cream
⅔ cup powdered sugar

Whip the cream, adding sugar, egg and vanilla.

Fruit Cocktail Crunch

1 egg
1 cup sugar
1 tsp vanilla
1 size 303 can fruit cocktail
1 cup flour
1 tsp cinnamon
1 tsp soda
1 tsp salt

Beat egg with sugar. Add flavoring, fruit cocktail and sifted dry ingredients. Stir just enough to mix thoroughly. Pour into greased pan, size 8 × 12 inches.

Fruit Crunch Topping:

⅔ cup chopped walnuts
½ cup brown sugar

Sprinkle over top of batter. Bake at 325° for 45 minutes. Serve with whipped cream.

Prince of Wales Pudding

Since this appears in books of the 1930s, it must have been a favorite (or a dessert served to) Edward, Prince of Wales, who gave up the throne for love of Wallis Warford Simpson.

3 eggs
¾ cup sugar
2 T gelatine
½ pt sweet cream
Juice of 1 lemon

Dissolve gelatine in 1½ tablespoons cold water. Cream 3 egg yolks and sugar to a lemon color. Beat cream until stiff. To yolks and sugar add lemon juice, cream, stiffly beaten egg whites. Add ½ cup boiling water to gelatine, cool, and then add to mixture. Turn into mold and allow to set. Serve with whipped cream.

Apple Snow

Grate 1 large apple, add the white of 1 egg and ¾ cup of powdered sugar. Beat until thick enough to keep its shape as you pile it on the dish. A cup of mashed strawberries, peaches, or raspberries can be used in place of the apple. It is very nice used as a filling for layer cake or served as a dessert with a custard sauce.

King William Pudding

Two apples chopped fine, 2 ounces each of grated bread, sugar and currants; 2 eggs and the rind of a lemon, grated, and just enough of the juice to give a perceptible acid, a sprinkle of salt and a little mustard. Stir all together and pour into a small, buttered bowl. Cover with a plate and steam for an hour and a half; serve with lemon sauce made as follows: Boil together ½ cupful of sugar and ½ cup of water for 15 minutes; remove from fire and when cooled a little add the juice remaining from lemon used in pudding.

Tapioca Pudding

¾ cup large tapioca
1 qt water
2½ cups brown sugar
½ cup nuts
1 cup dates

Soak tapioca in water over night. In the morning add rest of the ingredients. Cook slowly until tapioca is done. Cool and serve with whipped cream.

Apple Corn Meal Pudding

Pare and core 12 pippen apples; slice them very thin; then stir into 1 quart of new milk 1 quart of sifted corn meal; add a little salt, then the apples, ½ cup sugar, 4 spoonfuls of chopped suet and a teacupful of good molasses, adding a teaspoonful of soda dissolved; mix these well together; pour into a buttered dish, and bake 4 hours; serve hot, with sugar and wine sauce. This is the most simple, cheap and luxuriant fruit pudding that can be made.

Baked Apple Roll

2 cups flour
2 tsp baking powder
1 tsp salt
2 T shortening
Milk
Chopped apples
1 cup brown sugar
1 tsp cinnamon
1 cup white sugar
1 cup water
1 T butter
1 T flour
½ tsp salt
½ tsp lemon juice or vinegar

Combine flour, baking powder, salt and blend in shortening. Add enough milk to make a soft dough. Roll out about 1 inch thick. Spread with chopped apples over which sprinkle the brown sugar and cinnamon which have been mixed. Put on dots of butter. Roll up like a jelly roll, slice about one inch thick. Place in pan. Dissolve the white sugar in the water and add melted butter. Add flour, salt and lemon juice. Pour this sauce over the rolls and bake until apples are done. Serve with cream.

Creamy Sauce

Cream ¼ cup of butter; add ½ cup of powdered or brown sugar, gradually, then 2 tablespoonfuls of milk and 1 tablespoonful of brandy, drop by drop. Need not cook. Serve warm.

Butterscotch Sauce

⅓ cup brown sugar
¾ cup syrup
1 T butter
1 T water

Combine all ingredients and cook for 1 minute. Sauce will be thin until cold.

Orange Sauce

1 cup sugar
4 tsp flour
Juice of 2 oranges
Pinch of salt
Grated rind of 1 orange
2 eggs
1 cup cream

Blend sugar, flour, juice, salt, orange rind and boil. Beat eggs and add to mixture. Cook until thick. Cool. Beat 1 cup cream stiff and add to orange mixture. Serve on white cake as a dessert.

Angel Food Dessert

1 qt milk
⅔ cup sugar
4 egg yolks
1 tsp vanilla
¼ tsp salt
2 T Knox gelatine
½ cup cold water
4 egg whites
1 pt whipping cream
1 angel food cake

Scald milk and stir in egg yolks and sugar which have been beaten together. Add salt and cook in double boiler until it coats a spoon. While hot add gelatine which has been soaking in cold water. Cool and add vanilla. Beat the egg whites and whipping cream. When custard begins to set, fold in the beaten whites and cream. Break an angel food cake into pieces the size of a walnut. Put in large pan in layers to set—first cake, then custard, then cake and custard. Cut in squares and garnish with whipped cream if desired. Makes 16 to 20 servings.

Strawberry Angel Food Dessert

1 three oz pkg strawberry flavored gelatin
1 ten oz pkg sliced frozen strawberries or prepared pie filling
1 T sugar
Pinch of salt
½ 10 inch angel food cake torn small pieces
½ pt whipping cream

Dissolve jello in 1¼ cups boiing water. Stir in filling, sugar and salt. Cool this until it begins to thicken.

Fold in the whipped cream.

Cover bottom of 9 inch cake pan with half the torn angel food. Pour over half the filling and cream mixture. Make another layer with the rest of torn angel food. Pour over remaining filling and cream mixture. Refrigerate 4 to 5 hours to set firm. Cut in squares and garnish.

Black Bottom Cheese Cake

1⅓ cups fine graham cracker, vanilla wafer or Zwieback crumbs
⅓ cup melted butter
⅓ cup sugar
1 box vanilla pudding and pie filling mix
1 envelope unflavored gelatin
⅛ tsp salt
2 egg yolks
1 cup light cream
1 cup milk
1 tsp vanilla
1½ squares semisweet chocolate
1½ cups creamed cottage cheese
2 egg whites
⅓ cup sugar

Mix thoroughly the crumbs, butter and sugar and press into a 10-inch pie pan or 9×9 pan. Chill while preparing the filling. In heavy saucepan mix the pie filling, gelatin and salt. Beat in the yolks, milk and cream; cook, stirring until mixture thickens and comes to a boil; add vanilla. Pour ¾ cup of hot mixture over the semi-sweet chocolate and stir to melt and blend. Pour chocolate mixture over crust and chill. Force cottage cheese through a food mill or sieve and beat into remaining pudding. If you have an electric blender, put cottage cheese in that and gradually add the pudding and blend until smooth. Beat the egg whites until frothy; gradually add ⅓ cup sugar, beating until stiff. Fold into pudding-cheese mixture and pour over chocolate layer. Chill until firm. Decorate with whipped cream and chocolate curls made by scraping a semi-sweet chocolate square with a vegetable peeler.

121

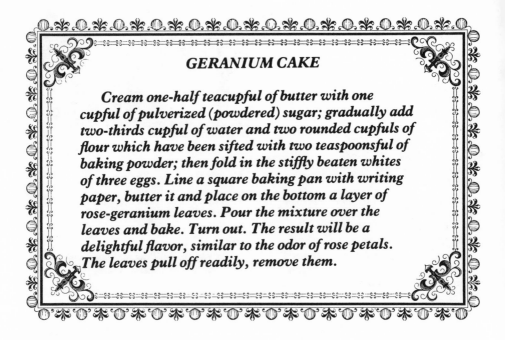

GERANIUM CAKE

*Cream one-half teacupful of butter with one
cupful of pulverized (powdered) sugar; gradually add
two-thirds cupful of water and two rounded cupfuls of
flour which have been sifted with two teaspoonsful of
baking powder; then fold in the stiffly beaten whites
of three eggs. Line a square baking pan with writing
paper, butter it and place on the bottom a layer of
rose-geranium leaves. Pour the mixture over the
leaves and bake. Turn out. The result will be a
delightful flavor, similar to the odor of rose petals.
The leaves pull off readily, remove them.*

Highland, As It Was

Cemeteries were an important part of the church picture in the past. Often the solemn graveyard was — and still is — part of the churchyard itself.

In the little rural community of Highland in Wright County, Minnesota, the small white church is long since closed but the cemetery, lovingly cared for, is still functioning. Elaine Peterson remembers that church where her parents, August and Josie Johnson, were married in 1908, possibly the first wedding in the church. And she remembers going to church there as a small child.

"Those sermons were very long, and they were in Swedish—I didn't understand a single word! I remember swinging my legs, which didn't reach the floor, until my dad squeezed my legs to tell me to sit still. I didn't like church too well in those days!"

But she remembers the Christmas programs when "the Christmas tree reached the ceiling and the candles were *real*. Bill Anderson paced around and around the tree all during the program to make sure the tree didn't catch on fire. He snuffed out the candles with a snuffer at the end of a long pole."

But there had been an even earlier church in Highland. Late in the 1800s three or four families organized a Quaker meeting house. Josie's friend Nellie Torgerson remembered it in a poem she wrote in the early 1940s, possibly after she retired from teaching in rural schools. It could be an elegy for all the long-gone country churchyards, the forgotten bridges and all the tiny hamlets across the prairies and wooded hills of the Midwest.

Do you remember Highland as it was?
The simple church, white, glistening in the sun,
The well-spaced windows, tall, on either side,
The door, a welcome step of broad-laid boards.

There was no steeple; the sturdy Quaker faith
Deemed better praise to God
The lofty elms, proud, swaying in the wind,
With wholesome maples, glory-splashed in fall.

Close by is seen the final resting place of those
Whose ardent plans and faithful toil
Had made this, their place of faith and worship,
The true endeavor of their lives.

The meeting house stood just atop the hill
Of waving woodland sloping to the river,
Whose sweeping curve washed banks of flowers and ferns.
'Twas here the old bridge spanned the stream.

From the hill past the church clearing
Came the rugged road,
Well-worn wheel tracks leading, now
Carefully, now easily, down the curving slope

Along the foot of the wooded height
To take the last steep slant of river bank,
Cross the bridge, and ease out on
Grassy bottom land

Where fragrant plum trees flourished,
With fruited grape vines swinging,
While near at hand—oh, roses, wild,
So pink and sweet!

These few lines I pen
For those within whose hearts
Still lies the treasured memory
Of lovely Highland, long ago!

Angel Pie

4 egg whites
1 cup sugar
½ tsp vanilla
¼ tsp cream of tartar

Whip egg whites until foamy. Add cream of tartar and gradually add sugar, beating constantly until thick. Bake in buttered pie tin (9″) for 1 hour at 250°.

4 egg yolks
½ cup sugar
3 T lemon juice
Grated lemon rind
1 cup whipping cream

Beat egg yolks and lemon juice until smooth and thick. Cook in double boiler until thick. Cool. Whip 1 cup cream, sweeten and flavor with vanilla. Spread ½ of cream on the baked meringue; then the lemon filling and finally the rest of the whipped cream. Top with coconut if desired. Let stand in refrigerator for 24 hours.

Chocolate Mint Dessert

½ cup butter
1 cup powdered sugar
2 squares unsweetened chocolate
3 eggs, separated
½ cup chopped walnuts
16 vanilla wafers, crushed

Cream butter and sugar, add well beaten egg yolks, melted chocolate, nut meats and mix. Blend in stiffly beaten egg whites. Pour into a 9×9 inch pan which has a layer of half of the crushed wafers on the bottom. Chill while preparing peppermint layer.

¼ lb peppermint candy, crushed
10 marshmallows cut fine
½ cup pecan meats cut
½ cup vanilla wafer crumbs
¾ cup cream, whipped

Add cut marshmallows to stiffly beaten cream. Add finely crushed peppermnt candy, vanilla wafer crumbs and nut meats. Mix well. Put on top of chocolate layer and cover with the other half of vanilla wafer crumbs saved from above. Chill 24 hours.

Chocolate Upside Down Cake

1 cup flour
¼ tsp salt
¾ cup sugar
2 tsp baking powder
2 T cocoa
½ cup milk
2 T melted butter
1 tsp vanilla
½ cup nuts

Sift the dry ingredients together. Then add milk, butter, vanilla and nuts. Pour into 10×6 baking pan and sprinkle a mixture of ½ cup white sugar, ½ cup brown sugar and 2 tablespoons cocoa over the top. Over this pour 1 cup cold water. Bake at 325° for 45 minutes.

Cranberry Holiday Dessert (Serves 16)

1 cup sugar
¾ cup shortening
2 eggs, beaten
2¼ cups all purpose flour
¼ tsp salt
1 tsp baking powder
1 tsp salt
1 tsp baking powder
1 tsp soda
1 cup buttermilk
1 cup chopped walnuts
1 cup dates (cut)
1 cup whole raw cranberries
Grated rind of 2 oranges

Pour following over cake after baked:

1 cup sugar
1 cup orange juice

Cream sugar and shortening, blend in beaten eggs. Sift flour and measure, sift with other dry ingredients. Add dry ingredients to creamed mixture alternately with buttermilk. Add walnuts, dates, cranberries, and orange rind. Bake at 350° for 1 hour. Pour combined sugar and orange juice over cake while still warm. Let stand 24 hours. Serve with whipped cream or hard sauce.

THE RANGE ETERNAL
With Its Thirty-One Particular Points of Eternal Excellence

Pineapple Squares

24 graham crackers
½ cup butter
1 cup sugar
1 cup sweet milk
2 tsp baking powder
½ cup chopped nuts
2 eggs

Cream butter and sugar, add beaten egg yolks. Roll graham crackers until very fine and add baking powder to crumbs. Add graham cracker mixture alternately with milk to the first mixture. Put in nuts and fold in beaten egg whites. Bake in moderate oven (350) for 45 minutes. Remove from oven and while hot, cover with a sauce made by cooking 1 cup sugar and 1 small can pineapple until thick. Cool. Serve with whipped cream. Serves 10.

Broken Glass Dessert

3 packages jello — one each of orange, cherry, and lime. Mix each in separate containers with 1 cup hot water and ½ cup cold water. Let harden. Heat 1 cup pineapple juice, ¼ cup sugar. Dissolve 1 package lemon jello in this mixture and add ½ cup cold water. Slightly thicken. Whip 2 cups cream and add and stir. Cut the pans of colored jello and mix all together in the bottom of 9×13 inch pan lined with graham cracker crust. Pour jello-cream mixture over it. Refrigerate until set.

Pumpkin Refrigerator Dessert

30 marshmallows
1 cup pumpkin
½ cup milk
¾ tsp cinnamon
¼ tsp ginger
¼ tsp salt
1 cup whipping cream
2 T powdered sugar
20 graham crackers
¼ cup brown sugar
⅓ cup melted butter

Stir together in double boiler the first six ingredients. Cook until dissolved. Cool 1 hour. Whip cream with the powdered sugar and fold into above cooled mixture. Make a crust of crackers, brown sugar and melted butter. Put more than ½ cracker mixture into a 9×9 pan. Pour in pumpkin filling and sprinkle rest of crumbs on top.

Favorite Pie Crust

3 cups flour
1 tsp salt
1¼ cup lard
1 beaten egg
2 tsp vinegar
5 T ice water

Sift together flour and salt. Cut in shortening. Combine egg, vinegar and ice water. Mix all together and roll lightly. Enough for two 2 crust pies.

Hot Water Pie Crust

1 lb lard
1 cup real hot water
4½ cups flour
4 tsp baking powder
1 tsp salt

Combine lard and hot water and stir until smooth. Sift dry ingredients and add to lard mixture. Mix well into a ball. Roll and add enough flour to handle. Keeps well in a tight container in refrigerator.

Pie Crust Mix

3 cups flour
1 cup shortening
1 tsp salt

Mix ingredients together.
For a two-crust pie:

2 cups mix
¼ cup milk
1 egg yolk
1 T sugar

Roll out and brush white of egg over it.

126

Favorite Pecan Pie

Cream together:

1 cup light Karo syrup
½ cup butter
½ cup sugar
2 eggs

Add:

¼ tsp salt
1 tsp vanilla

Coat with flour and add:

1 cup chopped pecans

Pour into pie shell. Bake at 250° until golden brown.

Carrot Pie

1 pt cut-up carrots
1 pt milk
3 T cream
4 eggs
1 cup sugar
1 tsp cinnamon
½ tsp ginger
1 tsp vanilla

Cook and mash carrots. Mix ingredients. Bake, cool, and serve with whipped cream. Makes 2 pies.

Nut Pumpkin Pie

3 cups cooked pumpkin
2 cups sugar
2 T flour
1 qt milk
1 cup nut meats
5 eggs
1 tsp cinnamon
1 tsp ginger
½ tsp salt

Mix flour, sugar, cinnamon, ginger and salt. Beat eggs and add the pumpkin and milk. Then add the dry ingredients. Cook until desired thickness. Cool. Add nuts, chopped, and pour mixture into baked shell. Serve with whipped cream. This makes two pies.

Cream, Coconut, Chocolate or Banana Pie

⅓ cup flour
2 cups scalded milk
2 eggs
¼ cup sugar
⅛ tsp salt
1 tsp vanilla
1 T butter

Mix dry ingredients; add slightly beaten eggs; add scalded milk slowly, stirring vigorously; add butter; cook 15 minutes in double boiler until thick. Cool and add vanilla; turn into baked crust and cover with meringue; brown in moderate oven. This fills one pie.

For Banana Pie, add 3 bananas.

For Coconut Pie, add ¾ cup coconut.

For Chocolate Pie, add 1½ squares chocolate.

Chocolate Pie

1 pt milk
⅔ cup sugar
2 egg yolks
3 level T flour
1 T butter
1 tsp vanilla
¼ tsp salt
3 T grated chocolate

Cook in double boiler, and pour into a baked pie crust. Cover with a meringue made from the whites of 2 eggs and 2 T sugar. Brown in a moderate oven.

Orange Cream Pie

1 cup milk
1 scant cup sugar
2 T corn starch
2 T flour
3 egg yolks
1 tsp butter
Juice of two oranges
Grated rind of one orange
1 tsp lemon juice

Oh-So-Good Pie

4 eggs
2 T butter
2 cups sugar
3 T vinegar
1 tsp each of cinnamon, allspice, cloves
1 cup chopped raisins

Pour in unbaked pie shell and cook slowly. It forms its own meringue.

Silver Pie

Peel and grate 1 large white potato into a deep plate; add the juice and grated rind of 1 lemon, the beaten white of 1 egg, 1 teacupful of white sugar and 1 cup of cold water. Stir well together and pour into a nice under-crust and bake. When done have ready the whites of 2 eggs well beaten, ½ a teacupful of white sugar and a few drops of lemon, all thoroughly beaten. Put this mixture on the top of the pie evenly and return to the oven to stiffen a few moments. When sent to the table just lay a teaspoonful of jelly on the center of each piece, to ornament, if you wish.

Apple Custard Pie

Two raw apples, ⅔ cup sugar, 1 tablespoon butter, a saltspoon nutmeg, 2 eggs, 1 cup of milk. Select large, juicy, nice-flavored apples, grate to a pulp, cream the sugar and butter, add the spice and beaten yolk of eggs, milk and apples. Line large plate with nice crust, fill with the custard and bake till firm. Beat whites with 2 tablespoons sugar, pile lightly on top and brown.

Apple Crumb Pie

Sliced apples
1 cup white sugar
Cinnamon
1 cup oatmeal
1 cup brown sugar
1 cup flour
½ cup shortening
¼ tsp salt

Butter a pyrex pie pan and put sliced apples in it. Sprinkle with white sugar and a little cinnamon. Mix together the oatmeal, brown sugar, flour and salt. Add shortening and mix till it forms size of peas. Put on top of apples. Bake 45 minutes to 1 hour in moderate oven until apples are done and top is brown.

Apple Cream Pie

1 cup chopped apples
½ cup raisins
1 cup sugar
1 egg, beaten
⅔ cup sour cream
Pinch of salt

Mix together and bake in unbaked pie crust until firm. Serve plain or with whipped cream.

Sour Cream Apple Pie

Sift:
2 T flour
⅛ tsp salt
¾ cup sugar
Add:
1 egg, unbeaten
1 cup sour cream
1 tsp vanilla
¼ tsp nutmeg
Blend until smooth. Stir in:
2 cups or more diced apples

Pour into unbaked pie shell. Bake at 400 for 15 minutes, then at 350 for 35 minutes.

Topping:
⅓ cup sugar
⅓ cup flour
1 tsp cinnamon
¼ cup soft butter

Crumble and sprinkle on top. Bake 10 minutes at 400.

Sour Cream Pie

1 cup sour cream
1 cup raisins
1 cup sugar
1½ tsp cinnamon
¼ tsp cloves
¼ tsp nutmeg
3 egg yolks, 1 egg white

Beat all together and turn into 1 pie shell, unbaked. Bake till firm. Whip remaining egg whites for top and brown in oven.

Sweet Cream Raisin Pie

1¼ cup sweet cream
3 T sugar
1 cup raisins
3 eggs, beaten
1 tsp vanilla
Pinch of salt

Put mixture in unbaked pie crust shell. Sprinkle a little cinnamon over the top. Bake in a slow oven.

Favorite Lemon Pie

Combine:

6 t cornstarch
1 cup sugar
¼ tsp salt

Add 2½ cups hot water slowly, keeping mixture smooth. Cook over direct heat, stirring constantly until mixture is thick and clear. Remove from heat. Add:

2 tsp grated lemon rind
⅓ cup lemon juice (2 lemons)
3 egg yolks, slightly beaten

Cook mixture almost completely. Put in baked shell. Top with meringue made from egg whites beaten stiff and sugar. Bake until brown.

Rhubarb Pie

3 cups rhubarb
2 cups sugar
3 T orange juice
3 egg yolks
3 T cornstarch
⅛ tsp salt

Pour boiling water over rhubarb and drain. Beat egg yolks well; add sugar, juice, cornstarch and salt. Pour over rhubarb. Put mixture in unbaked pastry shell, top with dabs of butter. Bake 10 minutes at 450°, then 30 minutes at 350° or when mixture does not coat the knife. Top with meringue made of the egg whites when pie has cooled somewhat, and bake 12 to 15 minutes at 350°.

Norwegian Lemon Pie

In 2 cups milk, mix 1 rounded tablespoon corn starch, and let come to boil. Then mix together 1 cup sugar, the juice of 1 lemon, 3 egg yolks. Add this to the first mixture and stir well; bake in unbaked pie crust until set, or about 30 minutes. Beat egg whites, adding ½ cup sugar, for top of pie. Place in oven and brown.

Heavenly Pie

2 bananas, mashed with a fork
2 egg whites, not beaten
1 lemon, rind and juice
1 cup sugar
1 cup whipping cream
1 baked pie shell

Add banana pulp to egg whites and beat until stiff; add lemon rind, juice and sugar, continuing to beat until it stands up in peaks. Pile gently in deep pie shell; bake till a delicate brown in very moderate oven. When pie is cool, whip the cream until stiff, sweeten, and cover pie.

Graham Cracker Pie

½ cup melted butter
25 graham crackers, rolled fine
1 tsp cinnamon
½ cup sugar

Mix all together. Keep 1 cup of mixture out for topping.

Custard

4 egg yolks
¼ cup sugar
1 T corn starch
1 T flour
2 cups milk
1 T butter
½ tsp vanilla

Meringue

4 egg whites, beaten stiff
½ cup sugar
Pinch of cream tartar

Grease pie tin and put first mixture in tin, then the custard, then the egg whites, and on top of all this, sprinkle the remaining cup of first mixture. Bake slowly for about 15 minutes.

Flapper Pie

12 graham crackers
¼ cup melted butter
½ cup sugar
Salt if oleo is used

Mix well, and use half of this mixture to line pie tin, saving balance for the top. For filling prepare the following:

3 level T cornstarch
¾ cup light brown sugar
2 cups milk
2 egg yolks
1 T butter
1 tsp vanilla

Pur cornstarch, sugar, milk, egg yolks and butter in double boiler and cook until thick. Add vanilla, cool. Pour into pie shell. Beat egg whites stiff; add 3 T sugar and continue beating; put on top of pie. Add remaining cracker mixture on top and brown 20 minutes at 350°.

Buttermilk Pie

Orange pastry
1 cup sugar
3 T flour
¼ tsp salt
3 eggs
2 cups buttermilk
4 T butter, melted

To make orange pastry, use orange juice instead of water and make like plain pastry, adding ½ teaspoon grated orange rind and 1 tablespoon sugar. Use to line a 10-inch pan. To make the filling, mix sugar and flour; add egg yolks and buttermilk, and then the melted butter. Fold in stiffly beaten egg whites and pour into pastry lined pan. Place in a hot oven (450°). Reduce heat to 350° F. and bake 45 minutes.

Cottage Cheese Pie

Combine and mix well:

1½ cups creamed cottage cheese
4 T melted butter
½ cup sugar
Grated rind of one lemon
2 egg yolks, unbeaten
½ cup washed raisins
¼ cup chopped walnuts
¼ tsp salt

Pour into a pastry lined tin. Bake 10 minutes at 500, then reduce to 350 and bake until firm and slightly browned on top.

Pineapple Sponge Pie

2 cups grated pineapple
2 eggs
2 T melted butter
½ tsp lemon extract
1 T corn starch
1 cup sugar

Beat egg yolks and sugar together with cornstarch. Add pineapple, lemon extract and butter. Fold in stiffly beaten egg whites. Pour into unbaked pie shell. Bake for 20 minutes.

Soda Cracker Meringue

2 eggs
¾ cup sugar
18 soda crackers
1 tsp vanilla
¼ cup chopped nuts

Beat eggs in small bowl until light and lemony. Add sugar, 2 tablespoons at a time. Fold in cracker crumbs, vanilla and nuts. Pour mixture into a buttered baking tin and bake 350° for 20 to 25 minutes. Do not overbake. This may be served with ice cream and fruit or the following topping:

10 marshmallows
¼ cup orange juice
2 cups fresh peaches, sliced
½ pt cream, whipped
⅓ cup powdered sugar
⅓ cup chopped nuts
⅛ cup chopped maraschino cherries

Cut marshmallows and pour orange juice over them. Let stand. Place sliced peaches over the baked meringue. Whip cream and fold in powdered sugar, nuts, cherries and marshmallow mixture. Spread over the peaches. Chill in the refrigerator at least 2 hours.

Calla Lilies

1 cup sifted flour
1 tsp baking powder
Pinch of salt

Beat 3 eggs until light. Add ¾ cup sugar gradually and beat well. Sift flour into eggs and sugar mixture in three parts and fold in. Add 1 teaspoon vanilla or almond extract. Drop from a large spoon on greased cookie sheet. Do only two at a time. Spread out thin with a spatula so they will be 5 inches in diameter. Bake in oven at 375° F. until they spring back when lightly pressed — about 8 minutes. Take off cookie sheet and shape into cornucopia or cone which looks like a calla lily. Fill with whipped cream and serve while fresh. (Some recipes suggest laying a narrow cut of orange peel on the cream for the lily's stamen.)

Black Bottom Pie

14 graham crackers
5 T melted butter
1 T gelatine
1¼ T corn starch
1½ T sugar
2 cups top milk
4 egg yolks
1½ squares chocolate
2 tsp vanilla
4 egg whites
½ cup sugar
¼ tsp confectioner's sugar
1 cup whipping cream
½ square shaved chocolate

Roll crackers, add butter and mix well. Pat out evenly in a deep 9-inch pan and bake 10 minutes in moderate oven. Soak gelatin in cold water. Scald milk. Combine 1½ tablespoons sugar with cornstarch. Beat egg yolks and add scalded milk slowly. Then stir in sugar and cornstarch. Cook over simmering water, stirring occasionally for about 20 minutes or until custard coats spoon. Remove from heat and take out one cup of custard. To this add melted chocolate and beat well with rotary egg beater. When cold, blend in 1 teaspoon vanilla and pour into cooled crust. Chill. While remaining custard is still hot, blend in gelatin. Cool but do not allow to stiffen. Make a stiff meringue by beating egg whites frothy, add cream of tartar and beat until stiff enough to hold a point. Then gradually beat in ½ cup sugar. Beat until very stiff. While the custard mixture is still smooth and soft, fold in the meringue and remaining vanilla. As soon as chocolate custard has begun to set, cover with fluffy custard and chill until set. Cover with whipped cream mixed with confectioner's sugar and sprinkle with shaved chocolate.

131

Punch, Candy

Holiday Punch

2 pkg cherry Kool-aid
¾ cup sugar
¼ tsp salt
¼ tsp nutmeg
½ tsp cinnamon
1 6-oz can frozen lemonade
1 can frozen pineapple juice
2 12-oz bottles chilled ginger ale

Dissolve Kool-aid in 4 cups boiling water. Stir in sugar, salt, nutmeg and cinnamon. Chill. Just before serving add frozen lemonade, pineapple juice and ginger ale. Serve on ice. Makes 2½ quarts.
qu01Punch2 46-oz cans orange-grapefruit juice
2 12-oz cans apricot nectar
2 quarts ginger ale
2 quarts pineapple sherbetServes approximately 50 people.

Punch for 150

4 cans frozen orange juice
4 cans frozen lemon juice
2 large cans grapefruit juice
2 large cans pineapple juice
4 large cans Hawaiian Punch
3 cups sugar
2 gallons ice water
6 each lemons and oranges, sliced
2 bottles ginger ale, add just before
    serving.

Hot Spiced Cider

1 gallon apple cider
1 cup brown sugar
1 cup frozen lemonade
1 cup frozen orange juice
1 T ground nutmeg
1 T whole cloves
1 T whole allspice (put in bag)
Orange slices

Combine ingredients in large kettle and simmer 20 minutes. Cool and remove spice bag. Serve hot or cold with orange slices floating in bowl.

Hot Cranberry Punch

Boil together 1 pound cranberries, 3 quarts water, 1 stick cinnamon, 12 whole cloves. Boil 10 minutes. Now boil juice of 2 lemons and 2 oranges and 2 cups sugar. Remove spices, combine mixtures, serve hot.

Percolator Punch

1 quart apple cider
1 pint cranberry juice
1 pint orange juice
½ cup sugar
1 tsp whole allspice
1 tsp whole cloves
3 cinnamon sticks

Pour liquids in percolator and put remaining ingredients in percolator basket. Perk normal cycle. Makes about 16 ½ cup servings.

Apple Juice Appetizer

2 cups apple juice
2 to 3 T sugar
⅛ tsp cinnamon
1 tsp lemon juice

Combine ingredients. Tint red if desired. Serve warm.

Orange Surprise

1 can (6 oz) frozen orange juice
    concentrate, thawed, undiluted
1 quart apple juice, chilled
Orange slices
Lime slices
Halved strawberries

Blend liquids and shake well. Pour over ice in tall glasses and add fruit to garnish.

The candy pages are often the most worn, spattered, smudged and tattered pages in the cookbook. This page from the 1924 "Tested Recipes" of First Lutheran Church, Sioux Falls, South Dakota, survived six children and countless cousins in the Edwin Ekstrand family.

Candy

Peanut Brittle

Mix 3 cups granulated sugar with 1 scant cup boiling water, and ¼ tsp. soda, let it melt over slow fire, cook gently without stirring until a little drop in cold water hardens quickly. Add 1 cup roasted, shelled and skinned peanuts with as little use of a spoon as possible. Turn the mixture into buttered pans and cut while hot. The brittleness of the candy depends much upon the scant use of spoon. Very good, but must be very careful in making it.   Mrs. O. S. Harum

Butter Scotch Candy

2 cups brown sugar, 1 tbsp. vinegar, 4 tbsp. water, ⅓ cup butter. Boil until it will harden when dropped into cold water. Just before removing from the fire, add a little soda. Flavor with 1 tsp. vanilla and pour into buttered tins to harden.

Mrs. Lewis Larson   Mrs. Chas. E. Brewster

White Taffy

2 cups white Karo syrup, 2 cups white sugar, butter size of an egg, 3 tsp. vinegar. Boil until the above threads. Chocolate may be added if desired for chocolate taffy, or nuts. Place on buttered plates and let cool. Pull until it is brittle, or will cut in pieces nicely, using large pair of scissors.   Mrs. J. O. Sholseth

Smith College Fudge

2 cups white sugar, 3 tbsp. cocoa or chocolate 2 squares, ⅓ cup white Karo syrup, 1 small can condensed cream, or ½ pt. cream. Mix all together and put on very slow fire to cook. When it forms a soft ball in water, remove from fire and beat real hard. Have ready 1 cup chopped English walnuts, 1 tsp. vanilla and a lump of butter. Add vanilla and butter as soon as removed from fire. Then when it starts to harden, add nuts. When it gets hard enough to handle, butter the hands and knead as you would bread, then form into a loaf and you can slice it off thick or thin. This is real creamy and will stay moist for days. If you have a chafing dish to make it in, it is much better as it cooks slower.   Mrs. O. M. Richardson

Mrs. Dale Howe   Mrs. W. Boyd

Fudge

2 cups sugar, 3 squares of Baker's chocolate, 1 cup rich milk. Boil until it forms a soft ball in cold water. Add 1 tbsp. butter, 1 tsp. vanilla, walnuts and almonds. Beat until it becomes stiff. Pour in a buttered pan, cut into squares. Viola Johnson Mrs. E. K. Skaro

Chocolate Fudge

3 cups white sugar, 3 tbsp. butter, 3 squares chocolate. Melt butter and chocolate over fire, add sugar, beat well until mixed, add ¾ cup milk. Cook until it forms a soft ball in cold water. Beat until cold and cut in squares.   Frances Thompson

109

Molasses Candy

One cup of molasses, 2 cups of sugar, 1 tablespoon vinegar, a little butter and vanilla, boil ten minutes, then cool it enough to pull.

Molasses Taffy

1 cup molasses
2 T butter
Pinch of salt
1 cup sugar
1 tsp vinegar

Mix molasses, sugar and butter and vinegar and boil until it threads when dropped from spoon. Add soda and stir well after removing from fire. Place in buttered pan and when cool enough to handle, pull until it becomes light in color. Stretch it into a long rope and cut with scissors into small pieces.

Divinity

3 cups granulated sugar
⅔ cup white syrup
⅔ cup hot water
2 beaten egg whites
1 tsp vanilla
½ cup chopped walnuts
Pinch of salt

In heavy large saucepan combine sugar, syrup, hot water and salt. Cook, stirring constantly till sugar dissolves and mixture comes to boiling. Cook to hard-ball stage (250°) without stirring. Pour hot syrup over beaten egg whites with continuous beating. Beat until quite stiff. Add vanilla and nuts and pour in pan or drop from spoon on oiled paper.

Bologna Sausage Candy

2 cups white sugar
1 cup milk
¼ cup butter
½ cup chopped nuts
1 pkg dates

Boil sugar and milk until it forms a soft ball in cold water. Add nuts, dates and butter and boil until it leaves the side of the pan. Beat until it begins to get firm. Roll like sausage on a cold wet towel. Serve in slices.

Peanut Butter Candy

3 cups sugar
½ cup milk
3 T light syrup
1 cup peanut butter
1 cup nuts
Flavoring

Cook sugar, milk and syrup until it forms a hard ball in cold water. Add peanut butter and beat until cool. Add nuts and pour in buttered pan. Cut into squares. Do not stir while cooking.

Mrs. Thompson's Creme Mints

2 cups sugar
½ cup white Karo
½ cup boiling water

Boil until it spins a long thread at 240°, about 10 minutes. Remove from heat and add ¼ teaspoon cream of tartar. Pour this over 1 beaten egg white and beat for 3 minutes. Add ¼ teaspoon peppermint. Beat until you can scoop it out in 5 little mounds of powdered sugar. Roll out in 3 long rolls and cut off pieces with a scissors.

Popcorn Balls

4 qts popped corn
1 cup dark corn syrup
1 cup sugar
1 tsp vinegar
2 T butter
⅛ tsp soda
1 tsp vanilla

Combine syrup, sugar, vinegar and boil until it reaches hard boil stage (248°). (I boil it ½ to ¾ minute). Remove from heat and add butter, soda, and vanilla. Stir. Pour syrup over popped corn a little at a time and stir until well coated. Shape into balls with lightly buttered hands. Cool.

Urban legends are stories told over and over in city settings. Unlike the usual legends, the events described are said to have happened in the recent past (though some of the legends have been circulating for years). There may or may not have been some truth in the original story, but in retelling it always happens to different people: "My cousin's secretary's husband . . .my neighbor's uncle's friend . . .a lady on the east side of town . . ."

For the past year I've been giving friends the recipe for a chocolate fudge supposedly made by a popular candy company. I explain, "A friend gave it to me, she'd gotten it from a sister-in-law in Arizona who knows a man who went into the candy shop and asked if they ever gave out their fudge recipe. 'Yes,' said the clerk, 'just fill out this form and we'll send it to you.' He got the recipe, along with a bill for $300. He paid the bill and now he's handing the recipe out to everyone he knows."

Now I find this "Candy Caper" listed among other urban legends, most of which concern haunted houses, people who lose limbs and other mayhem.

Could that be how Fanny Farmer candy comes to be listed in so many old books?

More likely the recipe is from The Boston Cooking School Cook Book, later to be known as The Fanny Farmer Book. That illustrious lady is credited with being the mother of level measurements. The story is told that when she judged a recipe contest sponsored by a flour company, she found that only five percent of the 800 recipes entered used reliable level measurements. Another story has it that one of her cooking school students pointed out to her that a "heaped teaspoon" could vary enormously. Whatever the instigation, Miss Farmer wrote her now-famous cookbook, calling for level measurements. And when Boston's Little Brown and Company turned it down, she paid for the printing of 3,000 copies herself. The book was revised 12 times, went through innumerable printings and is still in print today.

Fudge

3 T butter
2 squares chocolate
½ cup white corn syrup
3 cups white sugar
¾ cup milk
Add a little salt if desired

Brown the butter; melt chocolate in butter; add syrup. Then alternately add sugar and milk (1 cup sugar and ¼ cup milk). Repeat this three times until the amount is used up. Bring to a boil after each addition. Then cover to steam down crystals. Uncover and cook slowly until soft ball stage. Cool. Beat. Add vanilla and nuts. Important, always use a clean spoon each time you stir as to prevent possible crystalization.

— From a Twenties book

Heritage

Heritage Cooking

Rule Number One: There is only way to make the authentic food of your heritage, and that's to make it the way your mother made it, or your grandmother, or your mother-in-law, or the nice little lady who lived at the end of your block, or your uncle who owned the meat market.

For the foods of the past, the foods of the North European countries from which so many of us have sprung, are the foods of memory. We can still feel on our tongue the melting sheerness of the Christmas cookie; in memory we stomp the snow off our boots and open the door to the fragrance of Norwegian *lapskaus* stew on the stove, rich with the obligatory salt pork, pungent with whole allspice. Any deviation from what we remember is somehow "wrong."

But deviations there are.

Wanda Adams, food writer on the Seattle Post-Intelligencer, is of Portuguese extraction. She remembers eating a classic dish in a Portuguese restaurant and exclaiming, "But this isn't Portuguese! This isn't like Grandma made it!" On checking, she found that Grandma had never liked spicy food so she simply left out the fennel and coriander and other spices the traditional dish called for.

The fact that each cook tailored her dishes to suit her and her family's taste is brought out in the dozens and dozens of recipes for Norwegian lefse, Swedish limpa, Danish red cabbage, Finnish semla, German dumplings, nearly all of them with small variations. Origins of foods are cloudy, too. There are Finnish rye and Swedish rye, Norwegian meatballs and Swedish meatballs, Danish fruit soup and Finnish fruit soup, most of them indistinguishable from each other. There are more apt to be regional differences (as with the many kinds of lefse in Norway) than national differences. But most heritage foods are what they are because of the cook who passed on her recipe.

No less an authority than Julia Child says there is no such thing as a "real, genuine, authentic recipe" for just about anything, and we shouldn't worry about it!

Ingredients and methods are usually the same for classic national and regional dishes, but every cook gives personal style to a dish. If the general pattern follows tradition, she points out, who can say it's not authentic?

The only time being perfectly exact is important is if the dish was developed by a certain person, as in "Great Aunt Minnie's Delicious Head Cheese." Her word is law, says Julia, and you don't deviate.

Elsa Ellefsen, who heads a group of women who cook many ethnic banquets at the Nordic Heritage Museum in Seattle, knows as much about meatballs as anyone I've ever met, and hers are sumptuous. She doesn't reveal her recipe, but she'll tell you how she makes them fit the specific ethnic group scheduled for a given dinner.

"When I make Norwegian meatballs I mutter a few Norwegian words over them. And when I make Swedish meatballs I utter a few Swedish words over them. And when I make Danish meatballs, I sing the Danish national anthem."

Lefse, Kringler and Flatbrød

There is one food that is native mainly to one Scandinavian country—Norwegian lefse. (Though a recipe for "Swedish lefse" appeared in at least one book.) Different kinds of this soft flatbread were made in different parts of the country.

If you don't find one that reminds you of Grandma's, remember that, even within a category there might be infinite variations. For instance, in *Notes From a Scandinavian Parlor*, the late Marie Asheim recalls how her mother in Norway would brush lefse rounds with milk to give them a shiny surface; the milk must be from the first milking after a cow had calved. After the brushing with milk the lefse would be put back on the stove for further baking. It was packed away dry and softened by dipping in water before serving.

Krina Lefse

Heat 1 quart milk to the boiling point. Gradually stir in enough flour to make bread dough that can be kneaded and rolled thin. Bake on one side only on top of stove (or use 12-inch fry pan, or griddle). Spread out a flour sack towel and as the lefses are baked, stack them on the towel, folding part of towel between every two lefses.

Topping: 3 eggs, 1 tablespoon sugar, 1 pint cream (half and half). Mix these and add enough flour to make it of right thickness for spreading on each lefse. (One elderly Norwegian lady remembers that her mother added raisins.)

Run a Krina Comb (or a coarse white comb) over the topping on each lefse. (To make krina lines on it, line it well.) Put on cookie sheet and bake in oven until very light brown. Store in a covered box or tin can (will keep for months).

To serve: In a pan of warm water soak as many lefses, one at a time, as you plan to use. Remove from water. Butter each lefse well on plain side and sprinkle generously with brown sugar and cinnamon. Put two lefses together sandwich style and cut into pie-shaped wedges.

Hardanger Lefse

½ gallon buttermilk
1 cup sour or sweet cream
1 T soda
Salt to taste
Flour enough to roll quite thin

Bake on top of stove. Before serving sprinkle with water and when soft spread with butter and sugar. Cinnamon may be added if desired.

Milk Lefse

1 qt milk
½ cup cream
2 T shortening (scant)
2 T sugar
1 T salt
5 cups sifted flour

Boil first 5 ingredients. Pour hot on flour, and mix well. Roll out immediately and bake on top of stove. Makes 12 to 14 lefse.

Hard Lefse

2 eggs beaten with ½ cup sugar and ½ cup white syrup
1 cup buttermilk
1 tsp soda
Salt
Flour enough to handle

Roll thin and bake on moderately hot griddle. Before serving, moisten with water. Spread with butter, sugar and cinnamon.

Nordland's Lefse

2 cups buttermilk
2 tsp soda
1 heaping cup corn syrup
½ cup lard
Pinch of salt
Flour to roll thin

Bake on top of cook stove.

Lefse

2 cups mashed potatoes (hot)
½ tsp salt (scant)
1 T shortening
1½ cups flour

Combine the potatoes, salt and shortening. Cool and add ¾ cup of the flour. (Use the rest of flour on board to roll out.) Mix well and divide into 8 or 14 balls. Roll out thin on lightly floured board and bake on moderately hot griddle or lefse maker.

Potato Lefse

Boil 10 large potatoes, mash fine
1 cup sweet cream
3 oz butter
pinch of salt

Beat very light and let cool. Add flour to roll thin. Lay on hot cover of cook stove to bake a light brown.

Potato Lefse

8 good sized potatoes, cooked and mashed good. While still hot add ¼ pound or 1 stick margarine or other shortening and then let cool. Mix in enough flour to handle good. Mix a little flour in at a time. Take a little of the dough and see if you can roll it real thin, without it breaking into pieces. If it does, add a little more flour. Some potatoes take more flour than others. Fry on both sides in pancake griddle, over low heat until brown spots appear.

Kringler

Or kringel, cringler, kringla, klingler. A cookbook from Sweden lists "Kringlor;" a Norwegian book, "smakringle." ("small kringle"). These are both made from a typical sweet roll dough and twisted into figure-eights.

But those who contributed recipes to church cookbooks knew kringler in many forms: almost anything that was formed in a circle or rolled in a circle seems to qualify as kringler. (Kringler or kringlor is probably the plural form of kringla or kringle. Now, did you really want to know that much?)

Take your pick — any one of these will give you a satisfying treat:

Kringler

Mix together like pastry 1 cup flour, ½ cup butter, 1 tablespoon water. Pat into two strips about 3 inches wide on cookie sheet. Now heat to a boil 1 cup water, ½ cup butter. Remove from heat, add 1 cup flour. Beat in 3 eggs, one at a time. Add 1 teaspoon almond extract. When cool, spread on top of the two strips. Bake 45 to 55 minutes at 350°. Frost with 1 cup powdered sugar, 2 teaspoons butter and cream to make a spreading consistency. Cut in diagonal slices.

Norwegian Kringler

1 cup sour cream
1 cup buttermilk
1 tsp soda
1 cup sugar
1 tsp nutmeg
4 tsp baking powder
4 cups flour
1 tsp salt

Mix first four ingredients and add the rest sifted together. Knead dough lightly on floured board until smooth. Add a little flour when necessary for easy handling. Roll into strips about ½ inch thick and 5 to 8 inches long. Twist into pretzel or figure-eight shape. Bake until nicely browned, about 10 minutes in 450° oven. Serve like rolls, buttered.

Kringle

1 qt milk
1½ cups sugar
1 cup butter
1 tsp salt
2 envelopes yeast
Flour

Scald milk and cool. Mix dough as for bread, using necessary flour to make soft dough. Place in a greased bowl and cover. Let rise until double in bulk. Punch down and allow to rise 15 minutes. Roll like a lead pencil, form into rings or figure-eights. Place in pan and let rise as for rolls. Bake in hot oven.

Cringler

½ lb butter
2½ cups sugar
2 eggs
1 tsp vanilla
2½ cups flour

Soften butter, cream with sugar, add egg yolks and vanilla. Stir well. Add just enough flour to shape strips without them sticking to fingers. Dip in unbeaten egg white and sprinkle with sugar and cinnamon. Bake till done. (About 12 minutes at 350 to 375)

Kringler (Rusk Type)

4 cups flour
4 tsp baking powder
1 tsp salt
1¼ cups sugar
1 T crushed anise seed
2 cups half and half cream

Mix all together and let stand at room temperature for several hours. Using a floured board, roll bits of dough the thickness of a pencil and about 12 inches long. Take both ends, twist and form a bow, or knot. Bake at 325° about 20 minutes until light brown. Store in a cloth bag to keep crisp.

Kringel

2 cups sifted flour
1½ tsp sugar
½ tsp salt
½ cup soft shortening
¼ cup warm (not hot) water
1 egg, beaten
1 envelope yeast
½ cup milk
Apples, cherries or peaches, sliced
Cinnamon

Into large bowl sift flour, sugar, salt. Cut in shortening until like corn meal. Sprinkle yeast into water in small bowl. Stir until dissolved. Add along with egg and milk to flour mixture. Cover and refrigerate overnight. On lightly floured board roll half of dough into rectangle. Place fruit over dough and sprinkle with sugar and spice. Fold long sides to center over filling, pinch together. Slide kringel onto slightly greased cookie sheet. Prepare remaining dough in same manner. Bake at 400° 20 to 30 minutes. Spread with thin powdered sugar icing while still warm. (In another book a somewhat similar recipe is called "Danish Dringle".)

Knäckebröd

4 cups white flour
4 cups graham flour
3 cups buttermilk
1 cup sour cream
¾ cup sugar
1 cup shortening
A little salt
3 tsp baking powder
3 tsp soda

Combine liquid ingredients and stir, then add the melted shortening and the dry ingredients which have been combined. Roll out thin and bake in a moderate oven.

Flatbrød

1 or more cupfuls of boiling water
Butter, about 1 T to cup of water
A little salt
Flour

To the boiling water add the shortening, salt and enough flour to make a stiff sponge. Cool. Knead in enough whole wheat or graham flour (some prefer cornmeal) to make a stiff dough. Take small portions at a time and roll out very thin into round sheets, on a floured board or canvas. Bake on top of stove, turn the sheets, so as to brown them evenly on both sides. Put each piece in slow oven until crisp.

Cream Flatbrød

1 cup medium cream
Flour enough to make a stiff dough
½ cup sugar
A pinch of salt

Cut off pieces and roll out as thin as wrapping paper. Bake on top of a moderately hot stove. Sprinkle sugar on both sides as they finish baking.

Norwegian Flat Brød

2 cups buttermilk
1 cup cornmeal
1 cup graham flour
½ cup lard, add salt

1 cup corn syrup
2 tsp soda

Mix to a stiff dough with white flour, roll out thin and bake in slow oven.

Flat Bread

1 cup sifted white flour
1 cup dark flour

Heat 2 cups water. Add 1 cup milk, 2 T sugar, 1 T salt and 2 T lard. Pour over the flour. Roll as thin as possible and bake on top of stove.

Swedish Hard Tack

2 pkg dry yeast
2 tsp sugar
1 cup warm water
½ cup shortening
½ cup sugar
1 cup scalded milk
1 tsp salt
2 beaten eggs
6 to 6½ cups all purpose flour

Mix together dry yeast, 2 teaspoons sugar and water, let stand for 10 minutes. Melt shortening and sugar in the scalded milk, cool, then add salt and 2 cups flour, stir and add yeast and eggs. Mix well, add additional flour to make soft dough, add 1 cup at a time. Knead and let rise 1 hour. Cut into 12 portions. Roll out thin with rolling pin. Bake on cookie sheets in 400° oven, 3 to 4 minutes. Turn with spatula, and bake until light brown. Total baking time about 6 minutes. Cool on cake rack until crisp.

Rye Crisp

2 cups graham flour
2 cups white flour
2 T shortening (more of butter)
½ cup sugar
1 tsp salt, scant
1 cup sour milk, cream or buttermilk
1 tsp soda, dissolved in milk

Mix as for a pie crust. Add milk. Roll on canvas baking board. Bake on cookie tins. Imprint it.

Swedish Limpa

350°   1 hour   6 bread pans

4 cups buttermilk
1 tsp soda
2 cups water
2 cakes compressed yeast
3 T shortening
⅔ cup sugar
2 T salt
½ cup molasses
**Rye and white flour, equal parts, about
    6 cups each**

Dissolve yeast in ½ cup warm water,
adding 1 tsp sugar. Mix sugar, shortening,
molasses and water, and bring to a boil.
Add soda to buttermilk, then add hot
liquid mixture. Add rye flour. Mix well
and add yeast. Add white flour and knead
well. Place in greased bowl and let rise
until double in bulk. Turn out on floured
board, knead and shape into loaves. Place
in greased tins and let rise until double its
bulk. Bake.

Swedish Rye Bread

3 cups rye flour
1 qt warm water
1 tsp anise seed
2 T fat
1 T salt
½ cup sugar
¼ cup molasses
1 cake compressed yeast
White flour

Mix rye flour with water, shortening, fat
and sugar and beat. Add yeast softened in
warm water and white flour enough to
make a sponge. Let sponge rise three or
four hours. Add white flour to knead, and
let stand until double in bulk. Make into
loaves and let rise until double. Bake one
hour in a moderately hot oven.

Dark Rye Bread

Soften 1 cake yeast in ¼ cup lukewarm
water. Combine:

  cup brown sugar
¼ cup molasses
1 tsp salt
2 T shortening

Mix well and add:

1½ cups hot water
2½ cups rye flour

Beat well and add yeast. 1 tablespoon
caraway seed may be added if desired. Stir
in 3½ to 4 cups white flour. Knead well
and place in greased bowl. Cover and let
rise until double in bulk. Shape into
loaves. Let rise. Bake at 375° about 45
minutes.

A German Christmas Loaf (Strietz)

One and ½ pints of milk, full ½ pound of
butter, 1 cupful sugar, ¾ pound raisins, ½
pound currants, 3 ounces citron, 2 ounces
almonds after they are blanched and cut
fine, 2½ to 3 pounds flour, 1 teaspoonful
salt and ½ cake of compressed yeast. Set a
sponge ove night with 1 pint milk, about 1
pound flour, and the yeast dissolved in
water. In the morning add the butter and
sugar, rubbed in flour, the salt and 1 pint
of warm milk. Knead until the dough no
longer sticks to the hand, adding flour
gradually; lastly put n the fruit mixed with
a little flour. The dough should be as stiff
as bread dough. Let it rise again, and when
light, divide into small loaves which roll
out about an inch thick, lap over and put
on flat pans to rise again. When light bake
in a well-heated oven about ½ hour.

In Cokato, Minnesota, the town near which I grew up, the "town ladies" for the most part traded at L.E. Bergstrom's Corner Grocery, the Finns at the Farmers' Co-op Store and the Swedes with Axel Holmberg. Axel not only bought their eggs and hurried about the store picking up items as the farm wife read her list, but he talked Swedish with them. That was important.

Carlton Holmberg remembers clerking in his father's store. But there were women who would let no one but Axel wait on them. But patient as he was, even Axel's patience sometimes wore thin. Carlton remembers the woman who, after inspecting the beans and the prunes, demanded to know if the wooden matches in the box were good.

"Madam," Axel assured her, "I guarantee they are all good and there are enough to burn down both your house and your barn."

Every year Axel bought dry lutefisk by the truckload. It was piled like cordwood in back of the store and Axel cured it himself as needed. One year he bought and sold 1300 pounds. It was usually gone by Christmas.

Long before the store had any frozen foods case Axel sold frozen strawberries. "He'd get brave in the winter time and order them for the weekend," recalls Marie Holmberg. "He kept them in the back room where it was really cold. It must have worked out OK; his was one of the first stores to have frozen strawberries."

In the 1920s, when churches were beginning to change from all-Swedish worship services to English, old Swedish people poured out their concerns to Axel.

"Don't they know," complained one elderly customer, "that Jesus is Swedish and He won't understand?"

Smörkranser (Butter Rings)

1 cake compressed yeast
1 cup sweet cream
½ cup milk
4 T sugar
½ cup butter
3 egg yolks
1 tsp salt
3 to 3½ cups flour

Sift flour with 4 tablespoons sugar and 1 teaspoon salt. Add butter and mix until mealy. Scald milk and add 2 teaspoons sugar. When lukewarm add crumbled yeast and stir until dissolved. Add cream and beaten egg yolks. Stir this into flour mixing to a smooth dough. Place in refrigerator over night. Next morning make into twists, braids or coffee cake. Let rise ½ hour more and bake in moderate oven 350°. When baked spread with thin powder sugar icing.

Fastelavns Boller (Hot Cross Buns)

⅓ cup sugar
1¼ cup milk scalded
½ cu butter
1 tsp salt
2 eggs well beaten
2 cups flour
1 cake compressed yeast dissolved in ¼ cup lukewarm water

Combine all ingredients and beat until light and bubbly. Add, cup seedless raisins, ⅓ cup citron, ½ teaspoon cardamon, 2½ cups flour. Knead well; let rise and knead down. Make buns and bake 15 to 20 minutes.

Finnish Coffee Bread

1 cup milk
⅓ cup sugar
⅓ cup shortening
3 eggs
10 cardamom seeds, crushed
4½ cups flour
1 tsp salt
2 cakes yeast, dissolved in 1 cup warm
   water

Cream shortening and sugar. Add scalded milk and salt. Add beaten eggs and cardamom. Cool to lukewarm. Add yeast, flour and lightly knead on floured board. Let rise till double in bulk. Shape into braided loaves and let rise before putting in oven. Brush tops with lightly beaten egg whites and sprinkle sugar over. Bake at 350 for about 45 minutes.

Norwegian Christmas Bread

2 yeast cakes
1 T sugar
1 qt milk
1 cup melted butter
4 cups sugar
1 small box citron
1 small pkg orange peel
2 cups raisins or currants
8 to 10 eggs
1 large T crushed cardamom
Flour enough for stiff dough

At noon, place yeast cakes and a tablespoon sugar in a bowl with lukewarm water. At night add milk and flour enough to make a thick batter. Cover and let stand over night. In the morning, add other ingredients, make into a stiff dough. Let rise twice, kneading each time. Shape into loaves, let rise again and bake in slow oven for 45 minutes. Makes 5 to 6 loaves.

Svenska Skorpor (Rusks)

2 cups sugar
1 cup butter
2 eggs
1 cup milk
4½ cups flour

4 tsp baking powder
1 tsp vanilla
1 cup chopped almonds

Cream sugar and butter. Stir in eggs (one at a time) and beat hard. Add milk, flour and rest of ingredients. Divide batter into two parts. Roll into two long rolls in bread pans. Bake in a rather slow oven about 300°. When done and cold take sharp knife and cut into slices ½ inch thick. Lay flat in pans and dry in oven till light brown on both sides.

Kavring or Norwegian Rusks

4 cups scalded milk
1 cup shortening
2 cups sugar
1 cake Yeast Foam
Salt
10 cardamom seeds

Set at night, using enough flour to make a soft sponge. In the morning add one or two eggs, beaten, 1 teaspoon soda dissolved in hot water. Knead into stiff dough. Let rise and knead down again. Let rise and shape into biscuits, let rise again until double in bulk, then bake. The next day cut biscuits in halves and toast in very slow oven.

The Best of the Old Church Cookbooks

Are there really some "best" books? It probably depends on what you're hoping to find in them. For me, the discovery of many Scandinavian recipes—some very familiar, others completely unknown to me—was a pleasure. From that point of view I'd have to mention three:

The WMF Cook Book (second edition, 1939) of the Women's Missionary Federation of Plentywood, Montana, is brimming with basic recipes for sturdy, nourishing fare with some surprises thrown in like Stikkelsbær Grøt (Gooseberry Pudding). It has no Scandinavian section, but the Julekage and Smörbakkelse and all the rest reflect the heavily Norwegian makeup of the contributors.

My Favorite Recipes, put out in 1962 by the Augustana Lutheran Church Women of Immanuel Church, Almelund, Minnesota, puts its wonderful Swedish section in the beginning of the book. Mrs. C. J. Johnson's clear, easy-to-follow recipes for classic Swedish foods would make a fine book by themselves.

For many years now St. John Lutheran Church in Seattle has been selling *From Danish Kitchens,* a book made up completely of authentic Danish recipes, with titles printed in both Danish and English. The books continue to be available; write the church at 5515 Phinney Avenue, Seattle.

But one of the most intriguing books belonged to Adeline Sparling's grandmother, Randi Johnson of Little Fork, Minnesota. Its pages (86 of the 90 remain) are printed on heavy 8½×11-inch tagboard. The cover is gone and there's no other reference to title or year of publication. But the year is likely 1926; there's a full-page ad for Central Lutheran Church announcing that plans for the big new sanctuary have been approved and bids will be opened March 14. (The structure was built in 1927.) There's also a full-page photo of Anna M. Fardahl's piano and organ students and a mention of a 1925 first prize award for Miss Fardahl's composition, "The March of the Vikings," written for the Norwegian American Centennial.

The book may have been issued as a fundraiser for The Lutheran Inner Mission Society of Minnesota, which lists the year's accomplishments through its Family Welfare Department, Institutional Department, Settlement House, Employment Bureau, Summer Camp, Children's Receiving Home (Colony of Mercy) and Trabert Hall, girls' hospice and boarding club. Rev. H. B. Kildahl, president, noted that expenses for the year were $63,195 and "before the work can be extended the present heavy indebtedness must be removed."

Those were pre-merger days. A Twin Cities church directory on page 2 lists Lutheran churches from no less than 15 synods: Augustana, Buffalo, Danish, Eielsen, Finnish, Iowa, Independent, Joint Synod of Ohio, Lutheran Brethren, Lutheran Free, Minnesota, Missouri, Norwegian Lutheran Church of America, Norwegian Synod American Evangelical Church, and United Lutheran Church in America.

But they were moving toward inclusiveness. Central, said its full-page ad, "has from the beginning made a strong appeal to people of different synods and social antecedents all over the city." St. John's in Washburn Park called itself "The Mother Church of English Lutheranism in the North-West."

At the end is a section called "Foreign Recipes," heavy on such things as Norsk Julekage and Swedish Herring Salad. All recipes calling for flour specify Miss Minnesota Flour. Several of our Heritage Recipes are culled from this section.

Pressylta (Head Cheese)

Veal:
1 veal shank, meat and bones about 4½ lbs
7 tsp salt
3 bay leaves
2 medium onions, sliced
24 whole allspice
4 qts water
Pork:
4½ lbs pork shoulder meat and bones
7 tsp salt
3 qts boiling water
2 lbs fat pork
Head Cheese:
Veal stock, cooked veal, cooked pork and pork fat
1 tsp white pepper
1 tsp black pepper
1 tsp allspice
2 T salt, mix together
Salt Brine:
2 T sugar
1 cup salt
2 qts water

Veal: Add veal shank, salt, bay leaves, onions and allspice to boiling water. Cover and simmer until meat is tender, about 2½ hours. Remove meat from stock. Strain stock, chill meat and stock separately in refrigerator overnight.

Pork: Add pork shoulder and salt to boiling water, cover and simmer until meat is tender, about 2½ hours. Add pork fat the last hour of cooking. Remove meat and pork fat from stock, chill meat and fat. The pork stock is not used in the head cheese.

Head Cheese: Cook veal stock until it is cooked down to 8 cups. Remove gristle and bone from chilled veal and bones from chilled pork. Cut veal and pork in thin slices. Slice pork fat in thin slices as large as possible. Line 2-quart casseroles with cloth wrung out in hot water. Place slices of fat pork on bottom and sides of casseroles, covering cloths completely if possible. Add slices of veal and pork and lay them in alternate layers. Sprinkle each layer with mixed pepper and salt. Continue until veal and pork is used. Cover top with remaining pork fat. Pull cloths together as tightly as possible around meat and tie securely with string. Pour 1 quart of veal stock into each of two kettles and bring to boiling point. To each add one head cheese, tied in cloth. Stock should cover head cheese. Bring slowly to boiling point then cook slowly 5 minutes. Remove head cheese still in cloth to flat pan. Spread out ends of cloth smoothly over head cheese. Cover tops completely with bread board and on bread board place a 10-pound weight. Set meat in refrigerator and let weight press meat for 24 hours, then remove weight board and cloth.

Salt Brine: Add sugar and salt to water and bring to boiling point, let stand until cold. To store head cheese for several days, cover with cold salt brine and keep in refrigerator. Yield about 5 pounds head cheese.

Note: For the pork fat use fat sliced from fat pork roast.

—Mrs. C. J. Johnson

Editor's note: With today's freezers the salt brine step is eliminated. However, this classic method of preserving meat may have given a flavor and moisture to these pressed meats that we can't quite duplicate today.

Olivia Cole, growing up in Iowa, says no Christmas Eve was complete without lutfisk and Swedish meatballs at Grandpa's. "The first time I was in the kitchen when the fish was being cooked I insisted it was spoiled, from the way it smelled. But Mother said no, it always smelled that way, and sure enough, it tasted just as good. There have been many versions of the meatballs, but this is our present favorite. We make three- to five-pound batches and after simmering put portions in the freezer for later use."

Swedish Meatballs (Makes about 270 walnut-sized balls)

4 lbs lean ground beef
¾ lb pork sausage
2 cups finely minced onions
1 9½-oz pkg cracker meal
1 T dry mustard
2 tsp thyme
1 tsp baking powder
2 eggs
1½ cups scalded milk (cooled)
Salt and pepper as desired

Mix all ingredients together well. Roll in 1-inch balls. Place on foil-lined cookie sheet (with edge) and brown in 400° oven. Place in kettle of beef broth and simmer 30 to 40 minutes. Cool, skim off fat. Freezes well in broth. (Baking powder and simmering in liquid makes them very tender.)

Swedish Meat Balls

Grind together twice:
⅓ lb pork
1 lb beef
Add:
1 tsp salt
½ tsp pepper
½ tsp nutmeg
1 egg
3 T cornstarch
1½ cups milk or water

Knead for about 15 minutes, adding the liquid a little at a time as mixture becomes dry. Form into small balls and brown in

butter. Add 2 cups water, put on tight cover and let simmer for about one and one-half hours — until tender. Thicken the broth.

Norwegian Meat Balls

3 lbs meat, part pork
1 onion, small
2 eggs, beaten
1 cup sweet milk
1 cup bread or cracker crumbs
Juice of ½ lemon
2 tsp salt
1 tsp pepper
1 tsp ginger
1 tsp nutmeg
Mix well and fry brown.

One contributor to an early-day book assumed readers already had a working acquaintance with Norwegian meats:

Rullepølse (Roll Sausage)

Beef flank, broaden, sprinkle with salt, pepper, ginger, and onion. Roll, sew, cook in boiling water until tender; take out and press until cold. Serve cold.

More complete directions are found in the 1937 Women's Missionary Federation cookbook of Plentywood, Montana:

Rullepølse (Meat Roll)

Beef or veal flanks
Lean pork or veal
Salt, pepper, ginger, onion and other spices to suit taste

Trim flanks of excess fat and cut into convenient pieces. Season heavily. Spread onions and pork, cut into small pieces, on flank. Roll tightly and sew up firmly with strong cord. Wind each roll tightly with cord. Before putting into boiling water to cook, prick all over with a sharp-tined fork. Also prick now and then during the first fifteen minutes of cooking. Cook slowly from 1½ hours for veal to 2½ hours for beef. Cool under heavy weight.

Rullepølse (Mutton Roll)

One mutton side is cut into pieces 9 inches long and 7 or 8 inches wide. On each piece, place smaller pieces of veal or pork, preferably some of each. Sprinkle with finely chopped onion, pepper, ginger and salt. A tiny sprinkle of saltpeter will add a fresh color. Roll into oblong rolls and sew together. Make a solution of 1 lb salt and ¼ lb sugar, boiled in ½ gallon of water. When cool, pour over rolls. These can be kept about a month. When needed, take out of solution and boil tender. Put into a press overnight. Pull out threads and cut into thin slices for sandwiches.

Meat and Rice Balls (Koldalmar)

2 cups chopped meat (1 sausage and 1 hamburger); 2 cups boiled rice; seasoning to taste. Form in oblong balls. Cut the center out of a large head of cabbage; pour boiling water over it and let it stand 5 minutes until wilted. Wrap each meatball in a cabbage leaf, pack in casserole, and pour over it 1 can tomato soup thinned with 1 can water. Bake 2 hours.

For Koldalmas bake with ½ cup butter or drippings instead of tomato soup.

Kalvsylta (Jellied Veal Loaf)

3 lbs breast of veal
1 onion, sliced
½ cup diced celery
3 small bay leaves
6 whole cloves
8 whole allspice
1 T salt
3 cups water

Place veal in saucepan, add remaining ingredients, cover tightly. Simmer until meat is tender, 1½ to 2 hours. Remove meat from stock, strain stock. There should be 2 to 2½ cups stock. When meat is cool, remove bones and white membrance, grind meat, return meat to stock and bring to a boil. Pour into loaf pan (4½ × 8½ inches), chill in refrigerator several hours or overnight. Unmold and cut in slices for serving. Yield 16 slices or 32 servings for Smorgasbord.

Labskaus

Slice round steak, cut in small pieces. Put in skillet and brown with butter, season with onions, salt and pepper. When brown, cover with water and let simmer till tender. Small piece of salt pork is sometimes cooked with this. Peel potatoes and slice into skilled with meat and cook till done.

Lapskaus (Norwegian Stew)

1 lb fresh beef, cut up
1 lb fresh pork, cut up
½ lb salt pork, cut up
1 medium onion, sliced
8 potatoes, diced

Cover the meat with water and simmer for an hour with a few whole black peppers, whole allspice and a bay leaf. When meat is tender add onions and potato. Season with salt and pepper to taste. Cook about 20 minutes more. Stew will be slightly thick; may be thickened more with a flour-water mix.

Swedish Potato Sausage

3 lbs ground pork
2 lbs ground beef
Raw potatoes (⅓ the amount of meat)
1 T salt
1 tsp pepper
½ tsp allspice
1 large onion

Grind raw potatoes and onion, mix with ground meats and spices. Stuff into sausage casings. To use, boil gently for 45 minutes or bake in 350° oven about 50 minutes. Prick casings with darning needle during cooking to keep them from bursting.

Norwegian Sausage or Pølse

To ¾ part beef use ¼ part fat pork. Grind the meat three times, adding some onion, salt, pepper, nutmeg and flour. Moisten with broth made by cooking the scraps and bones of the meat. Use hands to work in the broth and seasonings until the mixture is spongy. If you do not have broth use water. Chill thoroughly before filling the sausage casings. These may be wrapped separately and frozen. (To use, thaw, then simmer or bake for an hour; serve with home-made mustard.)

Norwegian Meat Balls

2 lbs meat (⅔ beef and ⅓ pork)
½ cup flour
1 egg
Little chopped onion
Salt and pepper to taste

Mix, moisten with milk and cream, add egg and work fine. (The more it is worked the better they will be.)

Fish Balls

3 large fish (pike or pickerel)
3 eggs
1 qt milk
4 T corn starch
1 tsp ground mace
Salt to taste
2 T butter

Steak the fish, removing all bones. Grind the fish through meat grinder three times. Then beat with mixmaster, adding the eggs. Add milk gradually, dissolve the corn starch in about ½ cup milk and add to mixture. Add butter, mace, and salt. (More mace may be added if desired.) Shape fish with tablespoon and drop into hot fat in skillet. Fry on both sides until golden brown. (A mixture of butter and shortening for frying adds to the flavor.)

Finmarken's Fiskekaker (Fish Cakes)

1 6 pound pickerel (other fish may be used, but pickerel is preferable). Cut out the backbone and all the largest side bones. Remove skin. Put through meat chopper 5 times, salt to taste. 4 eggs, ½ cup butter, ½ teaspoon nutmeg and a little pepper, 2 tablespoons cornstarch or potato meal. Milk enough to make a stiff batter (about 1 pint), beat well. Fry like croquettes in plenty of fat. Dip tablespoon into cold water before putting it into the batter.

Norwegian Fish Pudding

Grind about 4 pounds of filleted pickerel in meat grinder 5 times. Work into this batter, ⅔ pound of soft butter and add 1½ quarts of milk, previously heated and cooled. Add the milk in cupfuls while working the batter. Then add 4 tablespoons of cornstarch, 1 tablespoon salt, and 1 teaspoon mace. Put in ½ pint cream and the whites of four eggs, well beaten. Put the batter in pans and set them in larger pans, partly filled with boiling water. Bake in oven (moderate) from 1–1½ hours. This will serve 12.

Kala Mojakka (Finnish Fish Chowder)

Any fresh fish
6 medium potatoes, cut small
1 cup celery, cut small
1 cup carrots, cut small
1 medium onion, chopped
⅔ cup rich milk
Salt, pepper, butter to taste

Boil the fish in salted water until the bones can be picked out. Fish heads and tails may also be used. Pick meat from bones. Boil vegetables until tender. Add fish and liquid in which it was boiled. Add the rich milk and bring to a boil. Salt, pepper and add butter as wished.

Lutefisk

Cut fish into 4 sections. Place in a kettle of cold water, add a little salt and gradually bring to a boil. The fish will then be done. If it is boiled too long it will fall to pieces. The fish will keep its shape better if boiled in a cheese cloth bag. Drain and serve with melted butter or milk gravy.

Baked Lutfisk

3 lbs prepared lutfisk, ready to cook

Cut prepared lutfisk into serving pieces, rinse and drain well. Place one layer deep with skin side down in large shallow baking pan. Bake in a slow oven (325) for 35 minutes. Serve with cream sauce. Yield 4 servings.

(Generally, Swedes spell it "lutfisk" and serve it with cream sauce; Norwegians spell it "lutefisk" and serve it with melted butter.)

Swedish Pea Soup

Dried peas 2½ cups, water to cover, add ½ teaspoon soda; boil 15 minutes or until outer skin has cracked. Pour off water, rinse in several waters. Put peas in kettle with 2 lbs spareribs, salt to taste, add water to cover; boil until peas are soft.

Corn brought ten cents a bushel when Olivia Cole was growing up near Albert City, Iowa, during the Depression. "It was more economical to use the dry corn on the cob for firewood in the kitchen range. Papa also rigged up a saw and grinder on an old car frame axel so he ground corn, wheat and rye for us and for others. We got to where we enjoyed corn meal mush from home-ground corn for our evening meal. Leftover corn meal mush, sliced and fried, with butter and syrup, was a treat for breakfast."

Yogurt burst on the scene in the 1960s. "The first time I tasted it," laughs Olivia, "I said, 'Why, that's just the old clabbered milk that Mother used to make for us on the farm!' Mother would fill a large stone crock with skim milk, stir in a half cup or so of sour cream for starter and let it sit until the far end of the stove until it 'set' or thickened. The solid curds would form on top. Being careful not to disturb it, she'd move it to a cold place until evening. Our favorite way to eat it was to ladle it out in cereal bowls and put cream, sugar and shredded apple on top."

But best of all, says Olivia, "we liked something we called 'filibunke.' We'd fill a glass with clabbered milk (both curds and whey) and stir it vigorously with half a teaspoon of sugar and a dash of cinnamon."

Most of the old recipes had their roots in the farm. This one, from the 1941 edition of Grandfield Lutheran Church, Sheyenne, N.D., is a reminder of the faithful family cows:

Norwegian Mulse, or Milk Soup

1 gallon milk at night, skim in the morning
1 gallon milk in the morning, bring to boil

Take first gallon of milk, heat, add one rennet tablet which has been dissolved in lukewarm water. Stir well after adding rennet. Set off stove. When set, take plate and skim off. Cut this into squares, add to boil milk. Let boil and repeat till all is added. Cook until fairly thick and brownish. Remove from stove. Put in cool place and serve cold.

The recipe is from Mrs. H.N. Hendrickson, Sheyenne. Anna Hought, 101, explained to me that a plate is the easiest thing to use in skimming off whey, and cutting the "set" milk in squares released more whey.

The book was reissued in 1985, the church's 100th anniversary. A whole new section has been added, with recipes like New York Style Cheesecake and Microwave California Vegetable Casserole.

Rommegröt

2 parts of cream to 1 part milk

Cook cream 15 minutes before adding flour, adding enough flour to make real thick; cook until butter comes and takes off as much butter as possible. Have milk boiling hot and add gradually to thickened cream mixture. Salt to taste.

Rommegrød Cream Mush)

Sour cream boiled and stirred constantly. Sift in flour until mush gets thick. Stir steadily till butter comes out. Skim off part of butter to be used as gravy. Add more flour and boiling milk until thick.

Flødegrød (Cream Mush)

2 cups sour cream
¾ cup flour

Bring sour cream to boil, add flour stirring constantly. Cook the mush until it is thick and the cream comes to top. Serve with sugar and cinnamon sprinkled over the top.

FOR THE KITCHEN

Hoosier Kitchen Cabinets

Florence Oil Ranges

Allen's Princess Ranges

All grades of Linoleum in well selected patterns.

High Point, N. C.

KESTER FURNITURE CO.

Havregryn Suppe (Oatmeal Soup)

Heat 1 quart milk to boiling point (May use part water if desired). Stir in ½ cup quick oats, ½ teaspoon salt and ⅓ cup sugar, and boil for a few minutes.

Danish Æbleskiver

6 eggs
1 cup sweet milk
1 tsp sugar
1½ cups flour
1 tsp baking powder
½ tsp salt

Beat the egg yolks well, add the sugar, milk, then flour sifted with the baking powder. Beat the whites of eggs stiff and add last. Bake in Monk's or Æbleskiver pan on top of stove.

Kropkakor, komle, klub, palt — they're all names for potato dumplings. there's even Kartoffelklösse, which is German:

Kartoffelknösse

Three cups mashed potatoes, 3 beaten eggs, ½ teaspoon sugar (scant), ½ cup melted butter, 2 tablespoons flour, a little nutmeg, a few bits of toast soaked. Make into a dough. Roll balls of it in flour, drop into boiling water; boil until they rise to the surface. Serve with liver or sausage.

Komle (Potato Dumplings)

1 qt grated potatoes
1 tsp soda
1 tsp salt
4 qts meat stock (salt pork)
1 cup oatmeal
1 cup flour
Salt pork (cooked)

Mix and use enough flour to form balls, placing a small piece of cooked salt pork in center of each. Drop into boiling meat stock and boil with a tight lid, about 15 to 20 minutes. Lift out as soon as done. Serve hot with cream or butter. When cold can be sliced as potatoes and fried.

Kropkakor (Using Boiled Potatoes)

2½ cups cooked, mashed potatoes (warm)
1 cup mik
2 cups or more of flour
1 tsp salt
1 tsp baking powder

Mix ingredients. Form in small balls and place a cube of salt pork or bacon inside of ball. Boil 1 hour in salted water.

Danish Dumplings for Soup

1 cup boiling water
½ cup butter
1 cup flour
4 eggs
½ tsp salt

Melt butter in boiling water, add flour, and cook over heat until it does not stick to sides of pan. Cool, add eggs, unbeaten, one at a time. Drop by spoonful into soup and cook 20 minutes.

Olivia Cole: "Mother baked pancakes on a round griddle that held seven large pancakes at one time. But sometimes — probably to save time — she made an oven pancake in a 9×13-inch pan. They're sometimes called Dutch Babies or Wooden Shoes. The closest I can come to what she made is a recipe in "Favorite Tested Recipes" put out in 1958 by the Ladies of Our Savior's Lutheran Church in Albert City, Iowa, except that that calls for fried pork in the bottom of the pan and I don't use that."

Oven Pancake or Swedish Baked Pancake

Beat 3 eggs together, add 3 cups of sweet milk. Add 2 scant cups of flour (more like 1¾ cups) a little at a time, beating well after each addition. Bake in hot oven until raised high and brown. (About 35 minutes in 425° oven.) It will fall when taken out of the oven. Cut in squares and serve with lingonberries, fresh stawberries or strawberry jam, depending on the season.

Finnish Baked Pancake

4 eggs
4 cups milk
1¼ cups flour
2 T sugar
Dash of salt

Beat eggs well; add milk. Beat in flour, sugar and salt; mix thoroughly. Pour batter into 2 well-greased 9×13×2 inch pans and bake at 375 for 25 to 30 minutes or until done. Spread butter on top and sprinkle with sugar. Cut in squarse.

Tunnpannkaka (Swedish Thin Pancakes)

3 eggs
1½ cups sweet milk
½ tsp salt
2 T melted butter
1 T sugar
¾ cups flour
½ tsp baking powder

Beat well the eggs, and add one cup of milk. To this add the salt, butter, flour, sifted with the baking powder. Stir into a smooth batter. Add remaining one half cup mik and bake on greased medium hot griddle in large thin cakes. This may be spread with jelly and rolled.

Swedish Pancakes

1 cup flour
1 large cup milk
3 or 4 T sour cream
4 egg yolks
4 egg whites
Salt to taste

Mix ingredients as for any batter. Fold in beaten egg whites last.

Cabbage Rolls (Finnish Style)

1 large head cabbage
1 cup rice
½ cup light cream
½ large ground pork
1 tsp caraway seeds
1 T salt
¼ cup bread crumbs
½ lb ground veal
1½ tsp salt
½ cup honey

Trim cabbage. Place whole into boiling water. Season with 1 tablespoon salt. Cook until almost tender. Drain carefully. Remove leaves. Leaves which are too small can be used in the filling.

Boil rice in 2 cups water until almost cooked, about 15 minutes. Rinse. Soak bread crumbs in cream and water. Mix meat, soaked crumbs and rice together. Add chopped leaves, 1½ teaspoons salt, 1 teaspoon caraway seeds.

Place ½ pound of stuffing on each leaf. Roll leaf, tuck in ends. Place rolls on greased casserole with fold downward. Brush lightly with honey and bake 350°. When rolls have turned a golden brown, pour on a small amount of boiling water. Cover and continue cooking (baking) 1 hour and 10 minutes. Serves 4–6.

Swedish Brown Beans

2 cups brown beans
½ cup sugar
1 T corn starch
1 tsp vinegar
1 tsp salt
½ tsp cinnamon

Soak beans overnight. Drain and cook until done. Add sugar, salt, cinnamon and vinegar. Simmer for twenty minutes, thicken with cornstarch before serving.

Rutabaga Pudding

5 cups mashed rutabagas
2 cups milk
2 well beaten eggs
½ cup sugar
2 T butter
Salt and pepper to taste

Put all ingredients together and bake in moderate oven for one and a half hours.

Ost Kaka

5 quarts milk, heated until warmer than lukewarm. Dissolve 1 tablet rennet in cold water. Mix 1 cup flour into rennet mixture. Put this into milk and let stand until curdled. Then drain away whey, stir in 4 eggs beaten, ½ cup sugar into cheese. Add 1 pint cream and bake in moderate oven.

Ost Kaka

Heat 1 gallon milk to lukewarm. Moisten ½ cup flour with a little cold milk. Dissolve 1 rennet tablet in a little lukewarm water, add rennet tablet to the milk, also the moistened flour. Let stand until cheese leaves edges of pan. Stir good and let it settle. Drain off the whey, not too dry. Break up the cheese and stir in 4 beaten eggs, 1 cup sugar, a little salt, 1 cup cream and ½ teaspoon almond extract. Stir it all together and bake it for one hour, in a moderate oven, or until done.

Mock Ost Kaka

2 8-oz pkg cottage cheese
3 eggs, beaten
1 cup sugar
2 cups sweet cream

Combine all together and mix well. Bake 1 hour in 350° oven.

Fruit Soup "Saft Suppe"

12 oz mixed dried fruits
½ cup seedless light raisins
4 cups water
2 cups orange juice
1 T quick cooking tapioca
¼ tsp salt
⅓ cup sugar
3 inch stick cinnamon
6 whole cloves

Remove prune pits. Cut mixed fruits into small pieces. Add ½ cup dried apples if not included in dried fruit. Combine all other ingredients. Simmer, covered, until fruits are tender, about 30 to 40 minutes.

Remove cinnamon and cloves. Serve hot or cold.

Prunes and light or dark raisins are also very good instead of mixed dried fruits and dried apples. Prunes do not have to be pitted or cut up and any kind of fruit juice can be substituted for orange juice.

Söt Suppe (Sweet Soup)

2 qt water
½ cup tapioca
1 cup raisins
4 T vinegar
1½ cup sugar
1 lb prunes
1 tsp cinnamon or cinnamon sticks
2 cups sweetened fruit juice (grape juice is very good)

Boil prunes and raisins together until well done. Then add all other ingredients and boil until tapioca is clear. This is a Scandinavian dish usually used on Christmas Eve.

Trondhjem Suppe

¼ cup rice or sago, 2 quarts water. Raisins to taste. Cook these until well done, then add juice of one lemon, sugar to taste, ¼ cup cream and 2 egg yolks, beaten. Do not cook after eggs are in soup. More or less sugar and lemons may be used if preferred.

Swedish Blueberry Soup

Add 1 quart blueberry sauce and ¼ cup sago to 2 quarts water. Let come to a boil. Add 1 tablespoon cornstarch mixed with a little cold water. Sweeten to taste and let boil ½ hour. Flavor with lemon juice.

Danish Aebleskiver

½ cup butter, ½ cup sugar, 1 quart of milk, 4 eggs, 3 cups flour, 1 yeast cake. Warm the milk and add the yeast dissolved in a little of the milk. Cream butter and sugar, add yolks of eggs beaten well. Add this mixture to milk, add flour and beaten egg whites. Set in a warm place to rise for two hours. Bake in aebleskiver iron.

Rice Pudding

1 cup raw rice
1 pt milk
Butter size of walnut
2 cups sugar
1 lemon, juice and rind
4 eggs, separated

Cook rice in salted water until tender. Drain. Combine milk, butter, sugar, lemon and egg yolks; add to rice and cook 10 minutes. Pour into buttered casserole; top with a meringue made of egg whites and bake in a slow oven 325 to 350° until nicely browned.

Marts Sne (March Snow)

One quart of whipping cream beaten until stiff, 6 ounces of sugar, the grated rind of 1 lemon and juice of 2 lemons. 1¼ ounce Knox Gelatin dissolved in a small cup of water. Beat all together, add chopped cherries and nuts. Serve with red berry juice, either strawberry or raspberry.

Bruna Pepparkakor

1 lb butter
2 cups white syrup
3 cups sugar
3 eggs
8 cups flour
1 tsp cinnamon
1 tsp cloves
1 tsp allspice
3 tsp soda
3 tsp orange peel, if desired

Boil butter, sugar and syrup for two minutes. When almost cold, add spices. When completely cold, add other ingredients. Roll thin, cut and bake.

Pepperkaker

¾ cup butter
½ cup sugar
½ cup molasses
1 egg
3 cups sifted flour
1 tsp each of soda, cinnamon, and ginger
½ tsp cloves

Cream butter and sugar; add molasses and egg. Sift dry ingredients and add gradually. Cover and chill thoroughly for several hours or overnight. Roll out on lightly floured pastry cloth to ⅛-inch thickness. Cut into desired shapes with cookie cutter and bake on greased tins at 350° about 8 minutes.

Spritz Cookies

1 lb butter
2 cups sifted powdered sugar
2 egg yolks
3 T cream
4¼ cups flour
1 tsp almond extract

Cream butter and sugar. Add egg yolks one at a time, creaming well after each addition. Add cream and flavoring. Lastly add flour and mix well. Put through cookie press on ungreased cookie sheet. Bake in 350° oven until done.

Spritz Cookies

Cream together ½ pound butter, ¾ cup sugar, add yolk of 1 egg, 1½ tablespoon sweet cream, ½ teaspoon almond flavoring and 2 cups sifted flour before measuring.

Sprute Cookies

½ lb butter
¾ cup sugar
2 egg yolks
2 cups flour
Vanilla

Put through cookie press. Bake on ungreased cookie sheets.

Spritz Cookies

Cream 1 cup butter and ⅔ cup sugar
Yolks of 3 eggs
½ tsp almond flavoring
2 cups flour (add more if necessary)

Press thru cookie press into desired shapes. Bake on cookie sheets in hot oven.

Swan and Josephine's Family

Between Cokato and Dassel, Minnesota, and a few miles to the south lies Stockholm and the lovely old brick country church, Salem Lutheran.

"When I was in first grade in Sunday School in Stockholm," writes Helen Munson Hagen, "I thought that Dassel had to be a tremendously evil town, because we always sang about it in church:

> Oh let me feel Thee near me,
> The World is ever near,
> I see the sights at Dassel.
> The tempting sounds I hear.

"Much later, after I learned to read, I discovered that the words were, 'I see the sights that dazzle.'"

Founded by Swedish settlers in 1866, the church's longest-serving pastor was Swan Johnson who, with his wife Josephine, lived in the stately old parsonage on top of the hill from 1906 to 1933 and there raised nine children.

Helen, daughter of the oldest of the nine, recalls how "for years, whenever Swan and Josephine's children got together as adults for a reunion, they would have such a good time telling stories about their growing-up years in the parsonage."

And stories there were: the time the twins, Ruby and Reuben, set the bedroom curtains afire and left to go for a ride with their parents. (The fire miraculously burned itself out.) Trimming the kitten's fur to make it look like a lion and, when the results were bad and Mother would discover it, drowning the kitten in the rain barrel; Ruth discovering Luther lying on his back by the barn wall. "What are you doing there?" "I just fell off the barn roof." "Oh." And Ruth went on to the hay mow to play with the kittens. The Christmases when Swan, who never allowed liquor to be served in the parsonage, would brew his annual Christmas "drycka" or Christmas ale and would invite the deacons for a Christmas meeting in his study. "Around midnight the deacons would leave for home, all feeling very light-hearted and friendly."

As grandchildren, says Helen, "we were bored and yawned ungraciously when these stories were being told by our parents. But now as adults we have decided to accept, and finally collect, the Parsonage Stories."

Helen calls her collection *Eight Might Have Been Enough.* Here are some excerpts:

Ruth had to go to the basement to get something for her mother. There was no light there so she lit a match and walked down the steps, not seeing too well. On the bottom step was a tub of pickled herring. Ruth accidentally stepped into the tub of herring and onions, pulled her foot out and went about her business.

The herring continued to be enjoyed at lunch each day.

An elderly unmarried relative came to visit for a few weeks, someone the kids didn't especially take to. They wanted to play a trick on her. They had an outdoor toilet that had a hook and eye to lock the door. The kids moved the hook over a half inch so the door couldn't be locked.

[After the children were grown] Josephine always sat alone in the front pew during services. She looked very dignified and fashionable in her Sunday outfit. Skirts were long at the time.

On this particular Sunday, she had hurried down the back stairs of the parsonage, where a few mouse traps were set.

At the first communion table, there was Josephine kneeling with a mouse trap firmly attached to the bottom of her coat.

There was a shed on the parsonage grounds that didn't serve any particular purpose. On a night before Thanksgiving, 1906, Swan kept a turkey in the shed overnight, slated for their Thanksgiving dinner.

From that night on, for the next 25 years, though no turkey ever set foot in it again, that shed was always referred to as The Turkey Shed.

Swan's sister Mary was married to a Baptist pastor, Rev. Nelson. They had two children, Reuben and Effie. Reuben and Effie were always mannerly and impeccably dressed in white when they came to visit the Johnson clan. They enjoyed their cousins. By the time they left for home their clothes were dirty and their manners had changed somewhat.

Mary looked out of the window one Sunday afternoon and nearly fainted. There were her two children running across the top of the barn roof with some of the Johnson boys.

"How can you stand to watch this sort of thing?" Mary asked.

"I never look out of the window," came Josephine's reply.

A Delco electric plant was installed in the parsonage to provide electricity. The batteries were charged by a gasoline motor. Swan never did learn to call it the "motor." Instead he would say, "I have to start the mortar."

When the Johnsons left the parsonage he showed the new pastor how to start the "mortar."

And for the next ten years Pastor Carlson also had to "go and start the mortar." He never called it a motor.

Rosettes

2 eggs, slightly beaten
2 T sugar
¼ tsp salt
1 cup milk
1 cup flour
1 tsp melted butter or oil

Add sugar and salt to egg. Add flour and milk alternately, beating only until smooth. Heat rosette iron in hot lard, drain iron slightly and dip into batter and fry until delicate brown. Dust rosettes with confectioners sugar. Bakes about 45.

This is the standard rosette recipe. Rosettes are more crisp and sheer if made with 2 tablespoons less flour or 3 tablespoons more milk.

Rosettes

2 T sugar
2 eggs
2 cups milk
1½ cups flour
Salt

Mix eggs and sugar, beat until light and thick. Add 1 cup milk, beat well; add flour and salt, rest of milk and beat again. Have rosette iron and lard quite hot. Bake until golden brown, cool and dip in sugar. Keep in a cool dry place.

Krumkaker

1 cup butter
2 cups sugar
2 cups milk
3 cups flour
4 eggs
1 tsp vanilla
1 tsp crushed cardamon seed

Melt butter. Add sugar and beat together until smooth. Then beat eggs and add to first mixture, mixing well. Add milk gradually and beat again. Add vanilla and cardamon seed and flour. Put one teaspoonful in iron at a time. Makes about 80 — keep in dry place.

Krumkaker

5 eggs
2½ cups sugar
1 cup butter
½ cup water
2½ cups flour
½ tsp baking powder
1 tsp vanilla

Cream sugar and butter thoroughly; add beaten eggs and water; add vanilla. Sift together flour and baking powder and add to above. Drop by teaspoonsful onto a heated Krum-Kage iron. Bake on top of stove, first on one side and then on the other. Remove from iron and roll into cone shape.

Krum Kaka

Whip:
1 pt cream

Add:
1 cup powdered sugar
1½ cups flour
3 T cornstarch

Fold in: 3 stiffly beaten egg whites and about 2 crushed cardamom seeds. Bake on special iron using about 1 teaspoon batter each time. Turn iron so heat is even on each side. When slightly brown, remove and roll on a table knife or wooden spoon handle.

Strull

1 cup sugar
½ cup butter
3 eggs
1 cup sweet cream
2 cups sifted flour
1 tsp baking powder
Vanilla

Cream well the sugar and the butter and add the beaten eggs. Add cream and the flour sifted with the baking powder. Add the vanilla. Bake in strull iron and roll on knife or stick while warm.

Sandbakkelse (smörbakelse) may be served with or without filling.

Filled Smörbakelse

1 cup flour
½ cup butter
3 oz pkg cream cheese
¾ cup brown sugar
1 egg
1 tsp vanilla
1 T butter
Dash of salt
⅔ c pecans

Mix together flour, butter and cream cheese, chill for 1 hour then pat down in smorbakelse tins. Mix together brown sugar, egg, vanilla, butter, salt, and pecans. Fill tins about ⅔ full, takes only about ½ teaspoon in each tin. Bake at 325° oven for 25 minutes. Cool 10 minutes and then take out of tins.

Sandbakkels or Sand Tarts

1 cup butter
1 cup granulated sugar
1 egg yolk
4 T thick cream
1 tsp vanilla
Flour

Cream butter and sugar. Add egg yolk and cream and 1 teaspoon vanilla. Mix well, add enough flour so it will not stick to hands. Pat into sand tart pans.

Sandbakkelse

1 lb butter melted and cooled to remove
  salt
1 cup sugar
1 egg and 1 egg yolk
3 to 4 cups flour

Cream butter and sugar; add egg and yolk. Gradually add flour. With floured fingers spread dough thin in sandbakkels pans. Bake in a 325 to 350° oven about 10 minutes. The finished sandbakkelse should not be white or brown but a delicate ivory-beige so that the delicate flavor is not destroyed.

Fattigmand ("Poor Man's Cakes")

4 egg yolks
4 T sugar
4 T light cream
4 T melted butter
2 cups flour
1 T lemon juice
½ tsp ground cardamon seed

Beat egg yolks until light. Beat in sugar, add cream and melted butter. Stir in flour and mix to a smooth dough. Let stand for 2 hours. Roll out very thin on pastry cloth. Cut in diamond shape, cut a slit in center and pull corner through. Fry in deep hot fat (370) until delicately browned. Drain on absorbent paper. Sprinkle with powdered sugar before serving. Yield 4 to 5 dozen.

Fattigmand

8 egg yolks
1 egg white
4 T sweet cream
4 T sugar
1 tsp ground cardamon
2 cups cake flour

Mix and roll out very thin. Cut into diamond shapes and cook in hot lard until very light brown. Drain on brown wrapping paper.

Fattigmans

3 eggs, beaten light
4 T sugar
6 T sweet cream
1 tsp vanilla

Use as much flour as liquid will take. Roll thin and cut in strips and fry in hot fat.

Fattigmand Bakkelse *(poor man's cakes) are also called* klejnar.

Sølvkage

Cream ½ cup butter with 2 cups sugar, ½ cup milk, beaten whites of 8 eggs, 1 teaspoon baking powder in ¾ lb flour, 2 teaspoons cream of tartar, stirred in milk. Vanilla. Bake 1 hour.

Grise Ører

3 eggs, a little sugar, flour to knead hard. Beat eggs, add sugar and flour. Roll out thin, cut the same as fattigman and fry in hot lard. Dust with powdered sugar. This makes between 50 and 60.

Jødekager (Jewish Cakes)

1 lb sugar, 1 lb butter, 3 eggs, 2 teaspoons baking powder. Flour for very soft dough, about 4 cups, keep the dough cool. Drop by teaspoonsful on greased cookie sheet. Bake until just firm.

Peter Cookies (Danish)

½ lb butter stirred with ½ lb sugar, ½ lb flour, ¼ lb crushed almonds, and 2 eggs. Drop on a pan with a teaspoon.

Danish Sukkerkringler

1 cup sugar, 2 eggs, 1 cup butter, 1 cup sweet milk, 2 teaspoons of baking powder, a little extract. Work this together with the flour until dough is stiff. Roll it out until quite thin and cut in narrow strips, forming them into figure "8" and dip in granulated sugar. Bake in hot oven.

Tapfkuchen (German)

4 eggs, 1¼ cups sugar, 2¼ cups flour, ¾ cup raisins and citron, 2 heaping teaspoons butter, grated rind of 1 lemon, 2 teaspoons baking powder, 1 large cup milk, pinch of salt. Beat eggs well, add sugar, grated rind of lemon. Mix well, then add raisins, citron and milk. Add the flour mixed with salt and baking powder. Mix well. Melt and cool butter, add to mixture and beat for 15 minutes. Turn into well greased and floured bread pan and bake in slow oven from 60 to 70 minutes. When done turn out of pan immediately.

Kraemmerhuse (Danish)

¼ lb butter beaten until creamy, stirred with ¼ lb sugar, ¼ lb white flour, add 5 whipped egg whites. Spread dough in pan and bake light yellow, cut while warm into squares and form into "Kraemmerhuse" or cones made of the squares. When ready to serve fill with whipped cream.

Scandinavian Swirls

1 cup blanched almonds, or macadamia nuts, finely ground
1⅓ cup confectioners' (powdered) sugar
1 egg white
¼ tsp almond extract
Candied cherries, orange peel, or nuts

Mix nuts and sugar in medium-sized bowl. Beat egg white slightly with fork in small bowl; add gradually to sugar mixture; blend well. Add almond extract. Put through pastry tube or drop from tip of teaspoon onto well-greased and floured cooky sheets. Decorate tops with candied cherries, orange peel, or nuts. Bake in moderate oven (350° F.) 15 minutes, or until golden around edges. Cool on wire cake racks. Makes 15 macaroons.

Berlinerkranser

2 hard cooked egg yolks
1 cup sugar
1 cup butter
2 egg yolks
3½ cup flour

Mash hard cooked egg yolks well. Cream butter and sugar, add egg yolks, add flour and mix until dough is very smooth. Roll, about 2 teaspoonsful at a time, to the thickness of a pencil. Form into a ring crossing. The dough is more easily worked when it is chilled. Dip each ring in egg whites (that have been beaten until frothy), then in sugar. Bake in moderate oven until lightly brown. Dough may be put thru a pastry tube to form a long rope, then cut and shaped into a ring.

Berline Kranser

3 hard boiled eggs
4 raw eggs
1 cup sugar
1 lb butter

Beat the yolks of the raw eggs with the sugar, then mash the hard boiled egg yolks. Mix with the sugar and raw eggs and mix with flour and butter. Beat the whites of the eggs. Roll out in small strings with fingers and make in wreaths. Dip the rings in the egg white and then into white or colored sugar and then bake in 350° oven, until delicately brown.

Berlin Kranz

2 cups white sugar, 1½ cups butter (wash out salt), ½ cup sweet cream, 3 eggs (yolks of 2 and white of 1); flavoring. Add flour enough to roll and shape; dip in whites and sugar and bake.

Christiania Wafers

3 eggs, 3 tablespoons sugar, 3 tablespoons cream, pinch grated cardamon seed, pinch of salt, flour enough to make a stiff dough. Roll out very thin, cut in diamond shape, and drop into hot lard. Turn until light brown.

Norwegian Butter Cookie

1 cup soft butter
½ cup powdered sugar
2 cups flour
¾ cup walnut meats
2 tsp vanilla

Mix in order given and roll in little balls. Flatten slightly with fork. Bake for 10 minutes at 325°.

Mandelkake (Almond Fingers)

1 lb butter or margarine
1½ cup sugar (mix well)

Add:

5 cups flour
1 egg
1 tsp almond extract

Shape into a roll about the size of a finger. Cut into 2 inch lengths. For trimming dip tops of bar (1) into slightly beaten egg (2) into sugar (3) into egg again (4) lastly into shaved almonds. Bake to a light brown. Makes 10 dozen. Temperature 350°.

Crystal Garden (A Depression days novelty)

4 T bluing
4 T water
T salt
1 T ammonia

Mix and pour over a piece of coal placed in a dish. Additional salt or drops of food coloring may be added as "growing" begins.

Specialties
Elk Creek–Chimney Rock
Lutheran parishes, Wisconsin
(This really did "grow" crystals that we imagined looked like stalactites and stalagmites. If you don't know what bluing was, there must be some grandmother near you who remembers!)

Swedish Almond Drops

½ lb almonds
1 cup sugar
1 tsp grated lemon rind
3 eggs
⅔ tsp cinnamon

Wash almonds, then dry in moderate oven.
Put through food chopper. Beat egg whites
until stiff, add sugar gradually. Fold in
almonds, lemon rind and cinnamon. Drop
by teaspoonful onto greased cookie sheet.
Bake about 15 minutes in a slow oven.
When cool, store in tightly covered jar.
These cookies will keep a long time and
will improve in flavor.

Havrekakor (Oatmeal Cookies) or Lace Cookies

2 egg yolks, beaten
1 cup sugar
1 tsp salt
2 tsp vanilla
1 cup rolled oats

Beat until creamy, egg yolks and sugar.
Add salt, vanilla and rolled oats. Beat well
and drop on greased pan. Bake 10 to 15
minutes in moderate oven.

Lace Cooky Curls

½ cup sugar
½ cup butter
2 T water
½ cup quick oatmeal
⅓ cup chopped blanched almonds

Combine all the ingredients in a heavy
skillet. Stir until butter is melted. Remove
from heat. Drop by slightly round
teaspoonful, about 4″ apart onto a
well-greased and floured cooky sheet.
(Bake only a few at a time because they
spread.) Bake in 350° F. oven until light
brown, about 7 or 8 minutes. Allow the
cookies to cool slightly before removing
them from pan with spatula. Place over
wooden spoon handle to make curled
shape. Very fragile cookie. Makes 3 dozen.

Old Fashioned Pie Crust Cookie

3 cups flour
3 T sugar
2 tsp baking powder
1 cup butter
2 whole eggs or 4 egg yolks
½ cup sweet cream
1 tsp vanilla

Sift together flour, sugar and baking
powder, then cut in butter. Blend in
remaining ingredients. Roll out on floured
board to ¼ inch thick. Cut in 1 inch wide
strips, 3 inches long with pastry wheel. Cut
in slashes and form semi circle. Brush with
slightly beaten egg white. Sprinkle with
crushed loaf sguar. Bake at 350° until
lightly browned.

Swedish Cookies

1 cup butter
¾ cup brown sugar
2 cups flour
2 egg yolks beaten
½ tsp vanilla
½ tsp maple flavoring

Mix, roll into ball the size of a walnut. Dip
into egg whites then into finely chopped
nuts. Indent center of cookie, bake 10
minutes at 375°. Indent again with handle
of table knife; finish baking about 10
minutes more. While hot put strawberry
jam or any kind of jam or jelly in center.

Krokaner

¾ cup sugar
1 cup butter
About 4 cups flour
2 egg yolks, beaten in measuring cup
Fill cup with cream to make 1 cup
1 tsp vanilla
Pinch of salt
1 tsp baking powder

Work flour, baking powder and butter
together. Add egg and cream mixture. Roll
out quite thin and cut into strips about 1
by 3 inches. Bake over bridge shaped tins.
Frost when cool.

Icelandic Cake

½ cup butter
1 cup sugar
3 egg whites (last)
1 cup milk
2½ cups flour
2½ tsp baking powder
1 lb raisins
Flavor with nutmeg and cardamom

Cream butter and sugar well. Add flour and milk alternately. Add raisins and spices, last the well beaten egg whites. Bake in loaf pan 9×13″, at 350° approximately 45 minutes or until done.

Danish Layer Cake

⅔ cup butter
2 cups all purpose flour
1 tsp baking powder
1 pinch salt
1 cup eggs (4 or 5)
1½ cups sugar
2 T milk

Sift together dry ingredients, add the sugar and cream together with butter. Beat eggs slightly and add to creamed ingredients. Add 2 to 4 tablespoons of milk just enough needed to spread batter into four 11″ cake pans. Bake in moderate oven.

Filling

1 cup water
¼ lb butter
4 T sugar
Pinch of salt

Put in saucepan and bring to boil. Dredge ½ cup sifted flour into boiling mixture with wooden spoon and cook over low heat until butter begins to ooze from dough, or leaves side of pan. Add 3 to 4 eggs, beat them in vigorously one at a time. Add flavoring. Fill cake with 2 layers of filling, center layer with red raspberry jam. Frost with boiled icing on top and butter cream at sides.

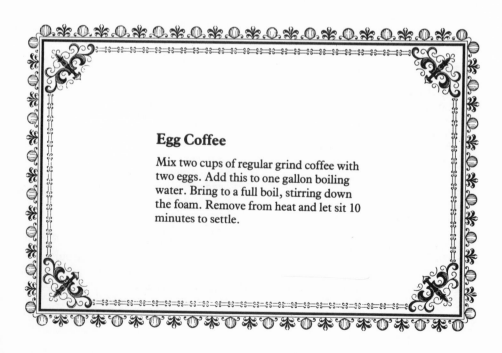

Egg Coffee

Mix two cups of regular grind coffee with two eggs. Add this to one gallon boiling water. Bring to a full boil, stirring down the foam. Remove from heat and let sit 10 minutes to settle.

A Treasury of Graces

For these and all Thy gifts of love,
We give Thee thanks and praise;
Look down, O Father, from above,
And bless us all our days. Amen.

God is great and God is good
And we thank Him for this food.
By His hand we all are fed.
Give us, Lord, our daily bread. Amen.

Heavenly Father, bless this food
To Thy glory and our good. Amen.

Come Lord Jesus, be Thou our guest
Let these Thy gifts to us be blest,
Renew our health and strength that we
May faithful in Thy service be. Amen.

Be present at our table, Lord,
Be here and everywhere adored.
These mercies bless and grant that we
May feast in Paradise with Thee.
Or: May strengthened for Thy service be. Amen

We thank Thee for these gifts, O Lord.
Feed our souls, too, with Thy Word. Amen.

Back of the loaf is the snowy flour,
And back of the flour the mill,
And back of the mill is the wheat, and the shower,
And the sun, and the Father's will.
                    M. D. Babcock

Oh, Thou, the source of all life's good,
We bow to thank Thee for this food,
And ask that we might feel Thee near
To help us live with hearts sincere. Amen.

Daily, O Lord, our prayers be said,
As Thou has taught, for daily bread;
But not alone our bodies feed;
Supply our failing spirits' need!
O Bread of Life, from day to day
Be Thou our comfort, food and stay. Amen.

I Jesu navn går vi til bord,
At spise og drikke på dit ord.
Gud til ære, os til gavn,
Så får vi mat i Jesu navn. Amen.
    (Norwegian table prayer)

I Jesu namn till bords vi gå
Välsigna Gud den mat vi få,
Välsigna detta kroppens bröd,
Och var oss när i liv och död. Amen.

För all din godhet och din spis,
Din milde Gud, ske tack och pris. Amen.
    (Swedish table prayers)

Roughly translated:

In Jesus' name we come to the table,
Eating and drinking in Thy name.
To God the glory, to us the gain.
So we receive this food in Jesus' name. Amen.

In Jesus' name we come to the table.
Bless, God, the food we receive.
Bless this earthly body's bread
And be near us in life and death. Amen.

For all Thy goodness and Thy food,
Oh loving God, (to you) be thanks and praise. Amen.

We praise Thee, our Heavenly Father, for these mercies provided for us. Forgive our sins, feed us spiritually, and save us in Thy service, for Christ's sake. Amen.

Grace our table, Lord, with Thy presence and add Thy spiritual blessing to these gifts that we receive from Thee. Amen.

We give Thee thanks, O Lord, for the gifts of food, friends and fellowship. Grant that Thy gifts may be used in the furtherance of Thy kingdom. Amen.

We thank Thee, Lord, for this our food,
For life and health and every good. Amen.

Let God be thanked whene'er is spread
A table with a loaf of bread,
For in each loaf these wonders hide,
And hungering folk are satisfied.

We thank Thee, for our daily bread,
Let also, Lord, our souls be fed;
O Bread of Life, from day to day,
Sustain us on our homeward way. Amen.

Ione Seastrand says that at the time of her marriage, she and husband Paul were given a copy of *Carolina Cookery from Quaker Kitchens,* published in 1924 by the Woman's Auxiliary of the High Point, N.C., Friends Church. "And all through our married life we have used this Quaker grace as a table prayer."

Whether we eat or drink, or whatsoe'er
We do or speak or think, let all be done,
Said, thought, in holy love and godly fear
Of Thee, our Heavenly Father and Thy Son!
That in the use of every good supplied,
The giver by his gifts be glorified.

A Trail of Glory

In *Huckleberry Finn* Jim observes the stars as he and Huck begin their float down the river. The small stars, he comments, fall to earth, leaving "a trail of glory."

There are few meteors among the contributors to these church cookbooks. They are small stars; many have "fallen to earth" long ago. But they have left a trail of glory. The glory still shines in church altar cloths, polished pews, in the lives of sturdy, honest, caring children and grandchildren and great-grandchildren. It shines in legislation they voted for and reforms they helped bring about, in hospital additions and mental health clinics. It shines in Third World countries where church outposts provide a distribution center for quilts made in the age-old methods of those mothers and grandmothers and great-grandmothers. It shines in the lives of their descendants who fight hunger, pain, violence and injustice in the name of Him who first set the stars in their courses. And it shines in the lives of all who see creative love as a channel—love that has made us what we are, love that can shape what is to be.

INDEX